Core Values in School Librarianship

Core Values in School Librarianship

Responding with Commitment and Courage

Judi Moreillon, Editor

LIBRARIES UNLIMITED®

An Imprint of ABC-CLIO, LLC

Santa Barbara, California • Denver, Colorado

Library of Congress Cataloging-in-Publication Data

Names: Moreillon, Judi, editor.
Title: Core values in school librarianship : responding with commitment and courage / Judi Moreillon, editor.
Description: Santa Barbara, California : Libraries Unlimited, [2021] | Includes bibliographical references and index.
Identifiers: LCCN 2020052147 (print) | LCCN 2020052148 (ebook) | ISBN 9781440878152 (paperback ; acid-free paper) | ISBN 9781440878169 (ebook)
Subjects: LCSH: School libraries—United States. | School librarians—Professional ethics—United States. | School librarians—Professional relationships—United States.
Classification: LCC Z675.S3 C756 2021 (print) | LCC Z675.S3 (ebook) | DDC 027.80973—dc23
LC record available at https://lccn.loc.gov/2020052147
LC ebook record available at https://lccn.loc.gov/2020052148

ISBN: 978-1-4408-7815-2 (print)
        978-1-4408-7816-9 (ebook)

25 24 23 22 21   1 2 3 4 5

This book is also available as an eBook.

Libraries Unlimited
An Imprint of ABC-CLIO, LLC

ABC-CLIO, LLC
147 Castilian Drive
Santa Barbara, California 93117
www.abc-clio.com

This book is printed on acid-free paper ∞

Manufactured in the United States of America

Contents

Acknowledgments

As the editor of *Core Values in School Librarianship: Responding with Commitment and Courage*, I had the honor of inviting school library and education leaders from across the United States to contribute to our book.

These passionate and compassionate contributors are my heroes. They committed to this project just ahead of school closures and persevered through the spring and summer of 2020 and into the unknowns as school districts prepared for and began the 2020–2021 academic year. The coauthors in this book are among the leaders who will assure the future of our profession for the benefit of all. I am in their debt for sharing their values, commitment, courage, and examples to follow.

All of the contributors to this book join with me in thanking the professionals who shared their experiences through the vignettes offered in each chapter.

We are also grateful for the support of our ABC-CLIO acquisitions editor Sharon Coatney without whose enthusiastic support this book would have never come to be. We are indebted to project editor Emma Bailey who shepherded us through the publication process.

Most of all, we are grateful to you, our readers. We thank you for pausing to reflect on your practice and recommitting to the core values and exemplary practices of our profession.

Judi Moreillon

Land Statement: The coauthors in this book have made their contributions from the homelands of seventeen American Indian nations. As the editor of the book, my writing and editorial contributions were made from my home in Tucson, Arizona, which is built on the traditional homelands of the Tohono O'odham and Hohokam peoples. Their care and keeping allows me to live and work here today.

Introduction: A Passion for School Librarianship

Judi Moreillon

> All school librarians need a firm foundation to provide strength and direction during these rapidly changing and challenging times.

Rapidly Changing and Challenging Times

These are indeed rapidly changing times. The pace of change led by technological innovation and global interconnectedness in every aspect of our lives creates a challenging context in which to learn, work, and live. The impact of change on the educational landscape is undeniable. Broadband, technology devices and tools, and digital resources have the potential to transform teaching and learning for students and schools with access. During the COVID-19 pandemic, the unconscionable digital learning opportunity gap for many K–12 students in the United States was exposed for all the world to see. As this book goes to press, long-needed strategies and initiatives to close this gap for students of all backgrounds, races, and socioeconomic status are still being considered, and funding for technology devices remains inequitable at the district, state, and national levels.

As author, reporter, and columnist Thomas L. Friedman notes in *Thank You for Being Late: An Optimist's Guide to Thriving in the Age of Accelerations* (2016), very few, if any, of us can keep up with the rapid pace of change. The accelerations in technology, globalization, and climate change result in the imperative to exist (and thrive) in a "constant state of destabilization" (Friedman 2016, 35). This requires flexibility, adaptability, and reflection. Although technology has made waiting obsolete, succeeding today requires patience—the patience to pause, think, and reflect, and the wisdom to adjust our priorities and actions.

We know that the current and future workforce requires and will require high-level literacy, technological skills, and continuous learning. But access to high-quality educational experiences is inequitably distributed. Whether face to face or in the virtual classroom, our increasingly diverse students bring their heritage and home cultures, their languages, and their need for social-emotional learning as well as academic learning to class every day. They also bring with them a call for justice. In locations across the United States, many school systems are failing to meet today's students' needs.

> *"The stakes are high for students who do not have access to information and digital literacy instruction. The stakes are also high for school librarians to raise awareness of the school library as essential to the education of all students."*
>
> —*Carol Gordon*

As educators in this challenging landscape, school librarian leaders are called on to bring our whole hearts, values, commitment, and courage to our work in order to best serve the evolving needs of all students, educators, and families. We must rise to our calling and lead our learning communities in seeking educational, racial, and social justice. We must demonstrate our core values and our value to the learning community. Finally, we must enlist the support of stakeholders in securing a role for librarians and libraries in the deeper learning our students need.

Friedman also points out that cultures must address people's anxiety about the present and the future. We must offer one another a "home." "It is so much easier to venture far—not just in distance but also in terms of your willingness to experiment, take risks, and reach out to the other—when you know you're still tethered to a place called home, and to a real community" (Friedman 2016, 452–453). In their daily work with students, other educators, administrators, and families, each author in this book is working to create a deep sense of belonging in their communities. We know the value of finding a "home" in the library—a place of possibility.

Finding a "Home" in Librarianship

I remember the day I found my "home" in librarianship. It was January 1990, on the very first day in my master's degree program. That day, with the guidance of my professor, I connected librarianship with the First Amendment to the U.S. Constitution. It was the day I realized the freedom of speech afforded all members of our society applied to K–12 students as well as adults. That day I understood it would be my job, as a school librarian, to ensure that students' voices had free expression throughout the school, community, and country. (Later, I expanded that view to the globe.)

It was the day I embraced my future work in the library field as "political." I learned about the political advocacy work of the American Library Association and our national association's Office of Intellectual Freedom. I saw my place in the education landscape as an activist. On that day, I, a classroom teacher, understood the potential of school librarians and libraries to have an essential role in elevating literacy, learning, and freedom in our schools.

But what I could not see that day was how the students with whom I worked would grow ever more diverse, how resources and tools for learning and teaching would increase beyond imagining, and how much of our global interconnectedness would impact our daily lives. I also could not see how the larger society would simultaneously constrain the freedom of students and educators through standardization; excessive testing; reduced federal, state, and local funding; and increased "choice" with the result of diverting taxpayer dollars away from district public schools.

Little did I know of the challenges my vision for equitable, effective, and compassionate library services would be put to over the years.

The Foundation: Core Values in School Librarianship

As educators, school librarians share values associated with classroom teachers, namely, a value for education as a pathway to success and learning as a lifelong endeavor. The contributors to this book focus on four core values in librarianship: equity, diversity, inclusion, and intellectual freedom. These are values school librarians share with librarians who serve in settings outside of K–12 schools. I would argue, however, that these four cornerstones of the library profession are most critical in school librarianship because we are often the only educator in our work environment who holds this specific combination of values.

> *"We are forever explaining why we're going out of our way to protect someone else's work, why it's important to consciously select diverse books, why the library is a safe place for everyone, and why we work so hard to protect our patrons' privacy."*
>
> —*Jen Gilbert and James Allen*

We are the single representative of the library profession to our stakeholders, so we must be clear and consistent in holding, sharing, and enacting these values. I believe that our core values in librarianship are *who we are* and are evidenced in *what we do*. They are our source of strength and power. When we remain true to our values, we can respond more effectively in tough conversations and difficult situations.

Through our exploration into core values in school librarianship and our commitment and courage in enacting them in practice, the contributors to this book seek to provide colleagues with a "home." When we are connected to others who share our values, we are able to provide security for one another and for our library stakeholders as we rise up to meet the opportunities and challenges of today and tomorrow. We will go out on a limb to enact our librarian values in our communities when we feel connected to one another—to our "professional home" in librarianship.

Working from the foundation of our core values and our unique position in our schools, we will colead alongside our colleagues to ensure that students, educators, administrators, and families benefit from the knowledge, skills, and commitment of state-certified school librarians as we go forward— together—to transform teaching and learning for all.

A Passion for School Librarianship Leads to Leadership

Author, speaker, and thought leader in education, Sir Ken Robinson (2013) reminds us of the importance of being a member of a tribe—a group of people who share passions and interests. When our relationships are centered around our passions, the people and ideas we work with become sources of inspiration and guidance. They can give us a new or renewed sense of what matters. Through interactions among members of our tribe, we continuously reinvent our identities. We revive our passion, commitment, and courage when they flag. We have support to remain true to our values and to act accordingly.

When we lead from the library as the center for literacy learning in our schools, our values will be tested. With the support of our tribe, we will rise up to meet these challenges for the benefit of the stakeholders we serve. "It is up to the leader to bridge the gap between doing and being, between dreams and actions that make those dreams real. Commitment and passion enable us to cross that emotional bridge" (Pearce 2013, 3).

The Need to Build Empathy and Take Action

The school librarian profession has been in "crisis" for more than a decade. Positions have been eliminated due to lack of funding and priorities that do not include school librarians and libraries. Many school librarians feel vulnerable, and others feel afraid. Whether those fears are real or imagined, guideposts are needed to offer today's school librarians a connection or reconnection to their passion for literacy learning and service that leads them or led them to the profession. This book of essays, quotes, and vignettes can provide some of the support school librarians need to lead and succeed at this time in our history.

Our library stakeholders must feel ownership in our libraries, our resources, and our programming. As R. David Lankes noted, "It is time for a new librarianship, one centered on learning and knowledge, not on books and materials, where the community is the collection, and we spend much more time in connection development instead of collection development" (2011, 9). As such, we must be able to build empathy—to be able to see our world through another person's experience. All of our library stakeholders must recognize their own cultures and experiences in the resources and programs we offer. If our communities appear to be homogeneous, it is our responsibility to provide library stakeholders with access to the vast diversity of the human experience through resources and programming that broaden their perspectives.

We must keep in mind that our local patrons are a part of a larger conversation—one that is global in scope. There is a compelling need for all of us to think of ourselves as members of an interconnected global society. Developing our own ability to express empathy for others and help others develop empathy are essential aspects of our work. As Friedman notes, caring ignites caring; empathy ignites empathy (2016, 152). As Chapter 3 coauthors Meg Boisseau Allison and Peter Patrick Langella demonstrate, school librarians cannot stop at empathy. If we are to build a just future, empathy must lead to compassionate action.

From Our Hearts to Yours

This book was written for all school librarians: preservice, newly practicing, and seasoned. In addition to being read and discussed in preservice education, the contributors believe our book will appeal to practicing school librarians who need extra support in enacting the core values of the profession at times when positions or budgets are threatened, during book challenges, school culture crises, administration changes, and other points in practice that test our values, commitment, and courage. This book could be given as a gift to be pulled off the shelf or from a bedside table to read and reflect on the critical importance of our unique contributions to school learning communities and by extension to the literacy world at large.

Brené Brown writes that daring leaders who live into their values are never silent about hard things. "Our values should be so crystallized in our minds, so infallible, so precise and clear, and unassailable, that they don't feel like a choice—they are simply a definition of who we are in our lives. In those hard moments, we know that we are going to pick what's right, right now, over what is easy. Because that is integrity—choosing courage over comfort; it's choosing what's right over what's fun, fast, or easy; and it's practicing your values not just professing them" (2018, 189).

> *"What comes from the heart enters the heart."*
>
> —*Talmudic Saying*

As literacy leaders, it is imperative for school librarians to periodically pause, to reconnect with our librarian values, to build empathy, and to take action on behalf of ourselves as well as our library stakeholders. Little did we know when we committed to this book that the COVID-19 pandemic and the Black Lives Matter movement would create a space and an urgent need to reenvision our future in school librarianship. As this book goes to press, there are many unknowns in the K–12 education landscape and in our profession. It is in this context that we offer this book. We, the contributors, offer inspiration, thoughts, and experiences as guides to help you lead in your learning community. We invite you to serve as models for school librarian values and to use your voice to affirm and enact them. We sing in the chorus behind you as you stand up today and tomorrow for and with the students, educators, and families in your care—for the hard things that can lead to social justice for all.

References

Brown, Brené. 2018. *Dare to Lead. Brave Work. Tough Conversations. Whole Hearts.* Vermillion: London.

Friedman, Thomas L. 2016. *Thank You for Being Late: An Optimist's Guide to Thriving in the Age of Accelerations.* New York: Farrar, Straus and Giroux.

Lankes, R. David. 2011. *The Atlas of New Librarianship.* Cambridge, MA: MIT Press.

Pearce, Terry. 2013. *Leading Out Loud: A Guide for Engaging Others in Creating the Future.* 3rd ed. San Francisco: Jossey-Bass.

Robinson, Ken. 2013. *Finding Your Element: How to Discover Your Talents and Passions and Transform Your Life.* New York: Viking.

PART I

Core Values in
School Librarianship

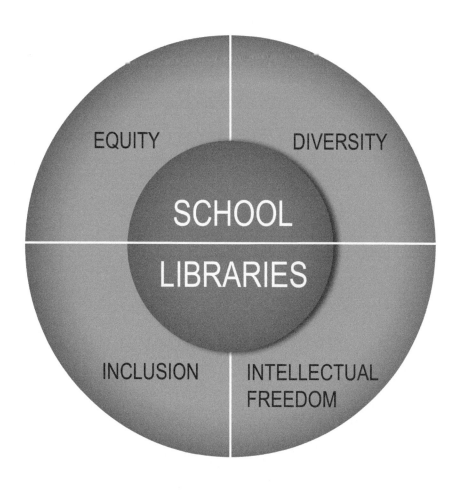

CHAPTER 1

Equity

Erika Long and Suzanne Sherman

Equitable access is a matter of social justice.

Based on experiences with graduate school classmates and colleagues in the field of school librarianship, we truly believe that you would be very hard pressed to find a school librarian who would be reluctant to immediately agree that equity should be paramount in all our endeavors. There are many in our ranks who are self-proclaimed social justice warriors and, yet, systemic policies, procedures, and preconceived notions, coupled with either the lack of knowledge or the tools to fully implement equitable practices in the field, create stumbling blocks toward reaching the goal. What we know for sure is that equitable access *is* a matter of social justice. The question we continue to work toward answering is whose role is it to push those stumbling blocks aside—or better yet, remove them altogether—so that attaining equitable access for all is achievable. A proposed answer: *you*.

You is a simple word that comes with a tremendous amount of responsibility, especially when considering doing social justice work. It is easiest to speak the words, write them on social media, or verbalize them in conversation, but the heavier burden comes with the sacrifice of putting those ideals into practice. But with passion, commitment, and courage, you can be part of a larger group of school librarians working to provide equitable access for every student not only in their buildings, but in their districts and the broader profession. Let's dig in to learn where the work begins.

With Passion Comes Purpose

I, Erika, never wanted to be in education. The thought of being responsible for a child's knowledge frightened me. I feared being to blame for someone not fully acquiring the information they required not only to pass a course but to also be successful in life. In my early thirties, that mind-set shifted. I reflected on the work I had done over the previous decade, and while I had spent my time in nonprofit and sports, the work I performed in those sectors essentially related to educating young people. This was the moment I realized being an educator was my purpose and that I had been passionate about it all along. I had become exhausted with working in a nonprofit and used what I knew about the collegiate student-athletes I worked with to determine my next career path. A large percentage of those young people lacked information literacy and digital literacy skills. My understanding that they had been denied a complete and appropriate educational experience is what influenced my decision to become a school librarian. My passion for access to education became my purpose.

School librarians love a great story. In our own origin stories, we share when and how we just *knew* we were destined to become school librarians dedicated to "getting the right book to the right kid at the right time." This mission is part of our very fabric. This noble calling generally leads us in the direction of pursuing either an MLIS or MIS, often at an ALA-accredited university. It is in these programs where theory and principles come into play and this abstract plan of providing access becomes grounded in pedagogy. In these contexts, courses like collection development and information retrieval become science. At times when exploring the theory leads to assignments and exams, our initial passion can be lost.

I, Suzanne, found this to be the case when I started this journey of transitioning from classroom English language arts teacher to school librarian. I had so much energy going into the program and a grand vision of just the kind of school librarian I would become. My first few classes in graduate school, however, provided a large dose of reality when I discovered just how much I had to learn about librarianship. I often felt inadequate in my understanding of the field as compared to many of my classmates who were already practicing paraprofessionals in academic or public libraries and who brought a great deal of experience to our course discussions. Doubt set in for me during that first semester as to whether or not I had made the right decision about pursuing my MIS as I attempted to make sense of this new environment that focused on access and retrieval. Once I settled in, however, and began to see how these topics were relevant to school librarianship and learned to translate the terminology into my own educational setting, I figured out a way to marry the principles of librarianship with my passion.

> *"Social justice refers to a concept in which equity or justice is achieved in every aspect of society rather than in only some aspects or for some people."*
>
> —*National Education Association*

Transforming Purpose into Pursuit

The charge of equitable access, to serve everyone in our community, dictates the social justice mission of librarianship. Most often, people automatically equate issues like climate change and human rights when discussing social justice, yet the right to access information is a human, constitutional right. Part of a librarian's purpose then should be the pursuit of equitable access for all. We see inequities throughout the profession—disproportionate funding and resources, lack of high-speed reliable Internet access, school librarian job cuts, school library closures, and more. All of these relate to access; who has it and who does not?

School librarians must be passionate about advocating for change when conditions prevent any student from benefiting from equitable access. As information professionals, it is imperative that we see beyond passion as it relates to providing experiences for learners in school libraries and accept the obligation to *ensure* equitable access. It is not enough to simply provide the right book for the right kid at the right time. Librarians have a duty to ensure every young person has access to *any* resource at *any* time and must commit to making equitable access a reality for all.

Commitment to Outreach

Librarians have widely been associated with protecting their patrons' rights and advocating for social issues in their communities. Our biggest responsibility has been to provide free access to information. During her career as a librarian, Dorothy Porter built "one of the world's leading repositories for Black history and culture at Howard's [University] Moorland-Spingarn Research Center" with a minimal budget (Nunes 2018). Although Porter aimed to curate and offer these materials for the purpose of "collecting and preserving . . . the global black experience," she also defied the Dewey Decimal System because it was a reflection of Whites' perception of the world. Instead, she catalogued the library's works by genre and author—an Africana method (Nunes 2018). Porter's insight and dedication to equity in retrieval and access are legacies that we all benefit from today.

In current times, we are tasked with having Porter's level of commitment and more because we are cognizant of where inequities lie. We cannot ignore or deny them. Of the 90,400 public and private schools in the United States, 61 percent of them have full-time librarians (Rosa 2019). In 2009, an American Association of School Librarians (AASL) survey found that 14 percent of respondents indicated that English language learners (ELLs) made up 25 percent or more of their school's demographics, yet more than half of respondents acknowledge that "their collections held none or less than 1% of non-English publications" (ALA 2010). Our commitment, then, must be to provide learners with equitable access to materials that meet their needs and interests even when doing so presents a challenge. For example, it is often difficult to procure materials in other languages, especially when seeking popular fiction for collections. If school librarians are to exhibit the type of commitment Dorothy Porter had, we must creatively discover means by which we can add materials in other languages—consider nonpopular titles in other languages, discover alternative vendors with a broader selection, opt for bilingual titles, and more.

> *"School librarians are equity warriors."*
>
> —Mary Keeling

It is critical that we use our passion to fuel action and fight to pursue social justice and dismantle the barriers that prevent equitable access in our school libraries. Others have done it before you; some quietly, others in much more radical ways. The point is, if you possess the passion, you will be compelled to commit to tackling this matter of social justice.

A great place to start is having a concrete understanding of the difference between equality and equity, as the terms are *not* synonymous. The American Library Association (ALA) declares, "Equity extends beyond equality—fairness and universal access—to deliberate and intentional efforts to create service delivery models that will make sure that community members have the resources they need" (ALA 2019). This has been historically true in our profession. Incorporating outreach efforts that move beyond the walls of the physical library can remove barriers to ensuring that all students have equal access to materials. Sharing print books throughout classrooms not only helps get more books into the hands of students who otherwise may not come to the library, but it also supports school-wide literacy efforts.

For me, Suzanne, my own creation of a bookmobile came out of desperation. When it became clear that high-stakes testing meant that our school library would be closed for days and weeks on end, I was frustrated. Students did not have access to physical materials, and nothing about this seemed right to me. One day, in the midst of this despair, I loaded as many "quick picks" and popular books as I could on a book truck and headed out into the hallways between classes to peddle our library's wares. I soon moved into the cafeteria, where I checked books in and out. I discovered that if I strategically parked myself and my cart with books during homeroom, classroom teachers would encourage students to come into the hall to check out books.

The next stage was to invite myself into classrooms with my cart. It worked, and soon our circulation statistics were up due to this effort. I continue to use the bookmobile in classrooms and have found that it can be a great benefit to students who feel overwhelmed by the sheer number of books when they visit the library. It also serves students who truly do not have the time to come to the library during the school day. Equity of access matters just as much as equity of materials.

School librarians in several districts in the country have continued to provide equity of access to materials throughout the summer by using bookmobiles. In 2017, school librarians from Gwinnett County, Georgia, launched a summer reading program on wheels with two mobile libraries named POW! and Explore! Over a span of eight weeks, more than 13,700 school library books had been put in the hands of preK–12 students, providing these students with access to materials that would have otherwise been unused during the summer break. In rural Arkansas, along with a literacy coach, school librarian Melinda Bailey, set out to deliver books in the Airedale Book Express in 2012 and has continued to expand on the success of the program each year (Ellison 2017). The legacy of taking books to the readers when they might not otherwise have them is rich, and these modern-day evolutions of those first pack-mule delivery systems continue to provide equity (McGraw 2017).

> *"Librarians are the revolutionaries of your environments. Librarians are the rebels, because what the librarian understands more than anybody is that you don't have to agree with the thing for it to exist on a shelf. There are things that librarians don't rock with but they understand that every book deserves to live."*
>
> —*Jason Reynolds*

VIGNETTE: FOR EACH AND EVERY ONE

Ali Schilpp

My love for school libraries and the students and families we serve was a call to action. In 2014, I became the first teacher-librarian to work at Northern Middle School, located in a small community school in the westernmost county of Maryland.

As I write this in the summer of 2020, I realize that living in a remote area has prepared us for the current pandemic. We social distance naturally due to our geographic location, and I personally have been doing so by "Accident" for almost six years. (I mean this literally and figuratively.) "Accident" is the name of the town where we live and work. There are no big box stores or chain restaurants. Anything of that sort, including bookstores, is at least 50 minutes away in any direction. Buying books from a Dollar General should not be your hub for literature. A lack of access to a third space is very prevalent in small towns, a space that only a library can provide. Currently, as we all quarantine, the library is dearly missed, and no amount of technology will replace our need for hands-on learning and a face-to-face social and intellectual place to be—together!

A hidden gem nestled among the Appalachian Mountains, our school was renovated in 2010 to become one of the most state-of-the-art schools I have ever seen. The design of the building is brilliant; the library is so spacious and bright. It is placed in the heart of the school where it should be. Only one thing was missing—a school librarian. After my interview, the school district made a progressive but overdue decision to provide a certified school media specialist. Can you believe that I was the only person who applied for what I consider to be the best job in the world?

I believe that so much depends on a school librarian working with every child and creating connections within their school community. I do not support the labels that are placed on kids in education. In Maryland, it is common for affluent suburbs and private schools to have school librarians; however, in large urban areas and small rural towns, school librarians are not always provided or have been cut "in tight budgetary times." These labels often reveal that certain locations do not always have a well-stocked or a staffed school library. I don't like to define anyone by one thing, especially where they are from. One could make so many assumptions based on our rural remote ranking. (Full disclosure: I am an unlikely representative of rural education. As a resident of Baltimore City for nineteen years, I am "not from here," but as a school librarian, it is my responsibility to provide for and support our school community. An advantage of coming from Baltimore was an abundance of public and private school libraries from which to gain inspiration and plan for my own school libraries.)

Now that I am serving students who attend a rural school, I am highly motivated to be the very best school librarian I can be. We all know that kids don't pick their zip codes or socioeconomic status, but serving this community has become my passion. As Jason Reynolds noted when he was named Ambassador for Young People's Literature, "I can't claim to love children if I only love some of them" (2020). I appreciate his focus on youth living in small towns and rural communities across our country since he is one of the most celebrated authors among my students.

A library does not stand alone, and nothing is accomplished alone. Anyone who connects with our students virtually and in-person has had an impact. Collaborating with other teacher librarians and peers abroad has made our library program engaging and exciting for students. The most rewarding moments in our library have been shared with authors and educators. I am so grateful for the days we shared with authors Ann Braden, Dusti Bowling, and John Schumacher. My students still mention their visits, and I am hopeful we will have those experiences again in the future.

Libraries can never be defined as one thing. They serve different purposes for each library patron and, I believe, are needed now more than ever, especially in schools with vulnerable populations. Internet connectivity has always been a challenge here in Appalachia. A benefit to our recent school closure was the fact that a survey revealed that over 30 percent of our students do not have Internet access. This forced the issue that connectivity was not a luxury but a right for all students.

In the spring, our district was awarded a grant from the Maryland State Office of Rural Broadband to provide hot spots for at-home, virtual learning. Students whose hot spots do not work in their homes are granted permission to work in the school building. Currently, my role as school librarian has shifted to preparing our teachers for virtual learning to support them as they provide online instruction from the building during the first quarter. Our school library is and will continue to be a hub for instructional and technology support—another great example of how school libraries benefit the whole learning community.

My mission for equity is to provide every child in our district with a school library and a librarian. I hope that our school library's success validates that having a certified school librarian improves the education and well-being of our students and school. I believe in the impact a school library has on every child as a place for them to make connections to literature and life. School librarians share the world of words, speak up for kids, and build their learning confidence. A librarian is the one educator in the school who works directly with every student. Each year/semester/quarter students' teachers change while the librarian remains a constant ally throughout their school years.

I have met some hardworking and dynamic librarians who truly love their library—and it shows. I hope that committed and effective school librarians will continue to inspire us and share their student success stories so more schools that have statistically less support, less digital access, and fewer books in the home, will work toward providing a high-quality library and dynamic librarian for their students. This should inspire school districts without a library program to provide one—for everyone.

Ali was School Library Journal *2018 Librarian of the Year and recently received the Children's Literature Advocate Award from Frostburg State University. She has been a certified school librarian for over eighteen years. Her work experiences include three different school libraries with students throughout Baltimore and Garrett County, Maryland.*

Equity during School Closures

Providing equitable access to materials, resources, and programming is highly important for librarians, and school librarians are no exception to this; however, when concerns over the spread of the COVID-19 pandemic suddenly closed schools across the country in the spring of 2020, the disparities in access became clear to our society as a whole. Mobile computers, high-speed Internet, and technology delivery systems allowed some school systems to continue providing educational services while others in effect ended the school year months earlier than scheduled. As Judi Moreillon (2020) points out, "It seems like an opportune time to, once again, reflect and wrestle with equity . . . or rather with the inequity of opportunity. . . . The technology gap that has plagued schools since the 1990s is tragically still alive and well. School districts are scrambling at this time to provide remote learning opportunities; at the same time, educators know that access to online learning will be inequitable." Even as school librarians have been acutely aware of these inequities, many citizens were unaware of just how unlevel the playing field has been for too many students.

In an effort to overcome the first barrier in online public education, reaching one-to-one device status, school systems across the nation utilized funding received from the 2020 CARES Act to purchase laptops and mobile devices for students. In addition to securing the devices themselves, school systems were also tasked with not only ensuring that students had access to high-speed Internet but also quickly bringing them and their teachers up to speed in how to incorporate best practices into online teaching and learning.

As I, Suzanne, suddenly found myself deeply entrenched in online training and seminars centered around providing instruction remotely throughout the summer of 2020, I recognized that now more than ever, I would need to ensure that all patrons had easy access to our digital resources and that my job also would include educating the faculty on how to best integrate these into their own classrooms both in-person and virtual for all levels of students. I began, first, to formulate a plan for how to best house and showcase the digital resources for optimal access for all 2,100+ students our library serves. I knew I had to consider password protection for databases as well as seamless integration into whatever platform our students would be utilizing in their academic courses. For me, this meant building a course in Canvas, which would be pushed out into each student's account. I found myself drawing from those graduate school courses in access and retrieval, merging theory and practice with passion in my pursuit of equity for students as they navigate these digital tools.

I initially began this task by searching for online tools to help me create interactive infographics that were already available and only needed my personal touches to lead students to the correct links for access to our local resources. The deeper I got into trying to find these, though, the clearer it became to me that design and attention to detail were going to need to be at the forefront in my efforts. The premade templates began to seem too busy and too cluttered to me, and it suddenly dawned on me that what I needed was something much cleaner and with much simpler access given that I would need to take into account our ELLs and special education students. At this point, I knew the task before me in terms of providing equitable access meant putting in the time and effort to build the infographics from scratch in order to meet all the different needs of our students.

As I set out to think through how to best design these interactive documents (mind you, I am *not* a trained graphic designer!), I continually asked myself how to best organize the information in terms of layout and design elements. I also determined how to layer access so that there were means to find basic information for all students and deeper layers of integrated links into more complex materials for the students in honors and AP courses. I was heartened and affirmed in these efforts as our ELL and special education department chairs presented training on best practices in universal design work found in an article by Karwai Pun (2016) entitled "Dos and Don'ts on Designing for Accessibility." I saw that my thinking and beginning efforts on accessibility were solid but now also had concrete examples to work with to ensure equitable digital access for the patrons I serve, including those with low vision and those on the autism spectrum.

Now that our district (Knox County Schools, Knoxville, Tennessee) will be one to one, in addition to providing access to online resources beyond the confines of the school buildings, we, school librarians, also have been given the opportunity to include more students in our readers' advisory efforts. As with designing entry points for our digital research resources, the necessity of creating new pathways to connect students with books is evident. In the fall of 2020 we were faced with the prospect of schools closing their physical doors and moving all students to virtual learning. Our own district selected a hybrid approach where caregivers had the choice of sending students back to school face to face or in a virtual classroom. This deepened the call for school librarians to ensure that students in both environments would be provided with equity in programming related to promoting reading for both academic and engagement purposes.

My school librarian colleague Rachel Smith reflected on this aspect of equity in the entirely digital environment by considering how to reach all Carter Middle School students. Her concerns were particularly for those who are often underserved, including but not limited to students in special education programs, ELL programs, or who are economically disadvantaged. Part of my work, then, became figuring out how to harness the power of our OPAC to help connect students with books (especially e-books) when I could not be there in person to do this. I knew that I would have to find a way to reach out to those reluctant and underserved students. The work in my OPAC looked like adding features to help students navigate and explore as well as ensuring adequate summaries were available in book records. Adding book trailers to bibliographic records allows students to preview books in a way that may feel more natural to them, as does ensuring that consistent and relevant subject headings are added to titles so that books can be found using the search terms kids are likely to use and understand.

Although access for all to both print and digital materials comes to mind first when considering equity, intentionally designing readers' advisory services to meet the needs of all patrons is just as important. Equity may also look like ensuring that patrons have access to these services when they need them most and not necessarily only when a librarian can be present in person with them. This has certainly become the reality for many of us as we navigate how to deliver services virtually, particularly when school systems adopt hybrid attendance plans where some students attend school physically while others have materials delivered solely online. Although most of us would argue that nothing can truly replace the experience for students of having a dedicated librarian working alongside them in the stacks to help them find the just right book at the just right time, the reality that distance learning has presented is that while ideal, this model may not always be possible.

> *"Philosophically, you have to have a disposition of questioning who's left out of the picture."*
>
> —*Kafi Kumasi*

Vignette: A Commitment to Equitable Access

Sarah Searles and Amber Moser

Seamless Integrated Access

The Knox County Schools (KCS) in Knoxville, Tennessee, is a large district serving about 60,000 learners and 8,000 educators. We, Sarah and Amber, are privileged to serve as the district's leadership and professional support for school librarians, with Sarah providing content area supervision and Amber providing instructional coaching. Throughout this vignette, "we" refers to our collaborative efforts to serve the district.

Among our schools, we have *every* kind of kid: our district includes antebellum wealth, urban poverty, rural farmsteads, and suburban sprawl, all within a few short miles. Even our ELLs are diverse; we have war zone refugees, the children of global executives, and a full spectrum in between. Serving all those learners effectively means providing them full and equal access to resources and the skills and supports necessary for using them efficiently. This is crucial to the fabric of our community because we expect every single one of our students to leave our schools ready to enter our local economy as productive participants with full personal agency.

One of our projects to help us ensure equitable access for all learners is a partnership with our local public library. The Knox County Public Library (KCPL) system hosts an annual, highly visible summer reading program. KCPL shares the names of students who completed the program with KCS librarians, and it is evident that students from our middle- and upper-class communities complete the program in far greater numbers than our students from lower-income communities.

Considering those data, we wanted to close that gap not only for summer reading but for more literacy learning broadly. We wanted every child to know that there are programs and materials available to them outside of school, and we wanted them to practice using those services so that they would develop positive habits and association with the local library system. This system has the capacity to allow our KCS students to pursue pleasure reading and learning beyond the school campus and to encourage them to continue using these services later as an adult. We wanted every KCS student to obtain and take full advantage of a public library card.

Students often face barriers in accessing public library services; they may not have transportation, and they likely don't have the freedom to physically visit a library branch. They don't necessarily have access to the documentation proving that they reside in the region served by the public library system. They may lack someone in their household who can complete the paperwork necessary for getting a public library card. We needed a process and some adjusted policies that would overcome those obstacles.

As a result of our public school libraries–public library partnership, these are the services KCS students now enjoy:

- In addition to a large print collection, the KCPL system offers thousands of digital items such as e-books, audiobooks, magazines, streaming videos, and databases.
- Students with a library card can access digital resources from a home computer or mobile device despite the limitations they may face in getting to a physical branch.
- All students, by virtue of being enrolled in a Knox County school, can forgo the documentation normally required to prove residency.

KCS and KCPL personnel worked closely to develop a routine system that would inform families that students were eligible to receive KCPL cards through a school enrollment process. No action was required of parents and guardians unless they chose to opt out of the service. Through mitigating barriers, KCS and KCPL have provided 24,627 students with KCPL cards, and our goal is to connect approximately 36,000 in the coming year.

Equity for the Underserved

We are also trying to focus on caring for our most vulnerable populations by extending school library access to learners who do not have professional school librarians in their schools. We are privileged in our district to have certified school librarians in every one of our traditional elementary, middle, and high schools (no small feat in a district our size), but we have several buildings that fall outside that staffing. These schools include standalone prekindergartens, alternative schools, and special education services. All are small facilities with modest and highly focused staffing formulas, which have not allowed them to hire librarians in the past. However, it is very important to our mission to ensure that the district's school library services truly serve every student. Therefore, we have looked for a variety of creative solutions to facilitate access in these schools.

Since our central office staff does not have the capacity to directly provide library services to these schools, our task is to build capacity among the building-level staff. Although these buildings do not have dedicated school library staff, each has educators who care deeply about their students' reading lives and are willing to go above and beyond to support their access to literacy learning. In various schools this might include the principals, teaching assistants released from other duties for a few hours per week, classroom teachers who freely donate their plan periods, or committees of volunteers. In all cases, we have coached and consulted with the building-level staff to help them set up their literacy spaces effectively, plan for how students will use the resources, and create a positive environment to nourish access.

Whenever possible, we look for ways to coordinate additional supports to meet the unique needs of these buildings.

- Occasionally, we have preservice school librarian candidates work on projects such as weeding collections that are typically formed from donations and are not necessarily high quality.
- Stipend funding has allowed us to hire certified school librarians for special projects like aligning schools' books to their preschool curriculum, or developing collection wish lists to use in their fund-raising efforts.

- Our district's maintenance office has helped us create positive and accessible environments with new furniture, refinished flooring, and customized shelving installations.

- School librarians generously donated extra copies and credit vouchers for the local used bookstore to build a young adult collection at one school.

- We realigned our budget to ensure all special schools would be included in our district-wide online resource subscriptions. Periodically, we provide staff training on how to access and use those resources.

- When one preschool was converted into a primary school, we convened a committee of volunteer librarians to catalog and automate their 3,000-volume collection in a single day.

We are clearing the way for more than 60,000 young learners to become lifelong learners. We are passionate about our commitment to undertake the work of facilitating equitable access district-wide as a point of social justice for everyone in our school community. Regardless of privilege, we will change lives. Our dedication to finding innovative ways to incorporate as many available resources into our delivery of services through building partnerships both in the community as well as creating more pathways for students to access resources has helped further our efforts to provide equity across the district.

Sarah is a library media services specialist for Knox County Schools (Tennessee). She is a Lilead Fellow and served on the AASL Board of Directors from 2016 to 2019. Sarah's upcoming book Explore *will be published by ALA Editions in 2021. Her articles on school librarianship have appeared in* Knowledge Quest *and* School Library Connection.

Amber is the facilitator for Library Media Services in the Knox County Schools. She has worked in education for twenty-three years and has served at the district level for six of them.

The Courage to Advocate for Equity

The first step in working to achieve equity within schools is ensuring that all learners in every school have access to a certified school librarian or district leaders who advocate for resources and services within underserved schools where this is not feasible from a staffing standpoint. Although these endeavors are outside the realm of what we as school librarians are hired to do, our own work toward providing equitable access for all includes remembering that we are called to serve all of our patrons equally, which means constantly being reflective in our practice and assessing regularly where adjustments need to be made to guarantee that equity is achieved. It takes courage to look inward and recognize where we may not be doing this, but evaluative measures are a necessary step in discovering these shortcomings.

Advocating for equity is an essential aspect of our jobs as school librarians. We enact it in a myriad of ways—including being vocal partners—in ensuring that students have equal access to technology and accompanying digital resources as well as collections containing books that interest them and reflect their experiences in the world. When our collection development practices demonstrate that we are working toward equity, we draw on Ranganathan's second and third laws where every reader has their book and every book has its reader (Rimland 2007).

Recognizing that for readers to be able to have the books that speak to them means creating collections that include works by diverse authors and illustrators and characters and events that mirror those in students' lives and experiences—even when those characters and events may seem controversial to others. School librarians must fight to include books that speak to readers despite the possibility of dissent. We must help all library stakeholders recognize the vital importance of incorporating a wide range of human experience in our collections. We must have the courage to stand up to potential challenges—for the sake of all students.

Reflection Questions

1. What steps will you take to ensure equitable access for all learners?
2. Think critically to discover which group(s) of learners lack equitable access. What or who can this be attributed to? How can you eliminate barriers to access?
3. Brainstorm services your school community lacks. Develop out-of-the-box ideas to meet these needs and create a time line for implementation. What barriers might arise, and how will you overcome them?

References

American Library Association. 2010. "AASL Survey Reveals U.S. School Libraries Lack Materials to Support Needs of ELLs." American Library Association, January 5. Available at http://www.ala.org/news/news/pressreleases2010 /january2010/survey_ells_aasl. Accessed October 1, 2020.

American Library Association. 2019. "Access to Library Resources and Services." American Library Association. Available at http://www.ala.org/advocacy /intfreedom/access. Accessed October 1, 2020.

Ellison, Jo. 2017. "Local Teachers Use Airedale Book Express Bus to Educate and Feed Hungry Kids." 5newsonline.com. Fort Smith/Fayetteville News/

KFSM 5News, June 14. Available at https://www.5newsonline.com/article /news/local/outreach/back-to-school/local-teachers-use-airedale-book -express-bus-to-educate-and-feed-hungry-kids/527-68723324-a6bb -47f4-bfd9-9608d28b8d87. Accessed October 1, 2020.

McGraw, Eliza. 2017. "Horse-Riding Librarians Were the Great Depression's Bookmobiles." SmithsonianMag.com, June 21. Available at https://www .smithsonianmag.com/history/horse-riding-librarians-were-great -depression-bookmobiles-180963786. Accessed October 1, 2020.

Moreillon, Judi. 2020. "Inequitable Access during School Closures." *School Librarian Leadership* (blog), March 16. Available at http://www.schoollibrarian leadership.com/2020/03/16/inequitable-access-during-school-closures. Accessed October 1, 2020.

Nunes, Zita Cristina. 2018. "Remembering the Howard University Librarian Who Decolonized the Way Books Were Catalogued." SmithsonianMag.com, November 26. Available at https://www.smithsonianmag.com/history /remembering-howard-university-librarian-who-decolonized-way-books -were-catalogued-180970890. Accessed October 1, 2020.

Pun, Karwai. 2016. "Dos and Don'ts on Designing for Accessibility." *Gov.UK*, September 2. Available at https://accessibility.blog.gov.uk/2016/09/02/dos -and-donts-on-designing-for-accessibility/?fbclid=IwAR23HdMReLa jg5Im4I3_5J31kOT99R8MeBBraMuYRdiWa5Ptg55FF9OI2us. Accessed October 1, 2020.

Reynolds, Jason. 2020. "Jason Reynolds Named Library of Congress' National Ambassador for Young People's Literature." *CBS This Morning*, January 13. Available at https://www.cbsnews.com/news/jason-reynolds-library-of -congress-national-ambassador-for-young-peoples-literature. Accessed October 1, 2020.

Rimland, Emily. 2007. "Ranganathan's Relevant Rules." *Reference and User Services Quarterly* 46: 24–26.

Rosa, Kathy S., ed. 2019. "The State of America's Libraries 2019: A Report from the American Library Association." *American Libraries Magazine*. Available at https://americanlibrariesmagazine.org/wp-content/uploads/2019 /04/2019-soal-report-final.pdf. Accessed October 1, 2020.

CHAPTER 2

Diversity

*Julie Stivers, Stephanie Powell,
and Nancy Jo Lambert*

Diversity in resources and programming is not optional.

Diversity: As a Foundation, Not an Add-On

Building, maintaining, using, and promoting a diverse, inclusive collection and library program takes both passion and purpose-driven work.

Julie: Issues of equity, diversity, and inclusion are foundational necessities for every school librarian. It is incredibly problematic that the education profession and our school librarian profession are overwhelmingly White and do not reflect our student populations. All school librarians must prioritize building diverse collections to become more culturally responsive educators for all of our students.

Championing diverse books for collections—and foregrounding the necessary accompanying equity work—cannot solely be the responsibility of Black, Indigenous, People of Color (BIPOC) librarians and librarians serving marginalized communities, including Black, Indigenous, Students of Color (BISOC). We recognize that diversity is much wider than race, but it is necessary for us to acknowledge the racism that exists in our world, country, communities, and schools and how this affects our BISOC on a daily basis. All school librarians regardless of the specific population they serve need to commit to this work with passion. It must be our shared purpose.

Nancy Jo: In *Dare to Lead: Brave Work. Tough Conversations. Whole Hearts*, Brené Brown says, "Daring leaders who live into their values are never silent about hard things" (2018, 184). Speaking as a member of the LGBTQIA+ community, I know how difficult it is for many school librarians to actively curate LGBTQIA+ collections and create programs inclusive of the LGBTQIA+ community.

I come to this work as a school librarian and educator from a place of privilege. I am a White cisgendered woman, and being a White woman affords me systemic privilege. No matter the struggles in my upbringing, I come from and operate in a place of privilege. That privilege has afforded me the opportunity to deny, or at the very least remain complicit in, systems of oppression. Without actively acknowledging this privilege, I cannot curate a truly diverse collection and create inclusive programming for my school library.

Stephanie: In this chapter focused on diversity, it is important for us to include points of view (POVs) that reflect the diverse populations that we, as librarians, serve. Through our three POVs, the lenses of our varied perspectives allow us to better understand how librarianship plays an important role in meeting those who we serve where they are and what they need.

Julie: We cannot expect labor from our BIPOC colleagues to educate us on this work. BIPOC librarians, educators, and authors have been leaders in championing diverse books for decades. Building diverse collections and library programs is a critical part of—and directly related to—our own personal equity journeys. Every librarian is at a different spot on this journey—the only constant being that we all must keep moving forward. Additionally, we all bring different life experiences with our own identity markers to this work. To demonstrate how the end goal—inclusive, reflective, diverse collections, spaces, and programs—is the same even though all of us come to this work at different stages, we're using unique POVs to show how we each tackle the theories, research, and strategies of this work.

Defining Diversity

We must bring purpose and intentionality even in how we define diversity.

Julie: Dictionary definitions of diversity often liken it to "variety." This surface-level definition highlights a pitfall for librarians when collecting resources. This shallow synonym limits our collection development and harms our students by likening diverse collecting to something that can be "'sprinkled" into our collections and onto our programs. If we focus on diversity as something extra, as something other, as something to be added to our collections and programs, we are unintentionally centering Whiteness—along with cisheteronormativity, Christianity, and monolingualism. For this chapter, we are instead adopting the definition of diversity used by We Need Diverse Books (2018):

> We recognize all diverse experiences, including (but not limited to) LGBTQIA+, Native, people of color, gender diversity, people with disabilities,

and ethnic, cultural, and religious minorities. We subscribe to a broad definition of disability, which includes but is not limited to physical, sensory, cognitive, intellectual, or developmental disabilities, chronic conditions, and mental illnesses (this may also include addiction). (diversebooks.org)

Benefits for All Students

> *"Research shows us that diverse books offer the following benefits to all students—increased academic performance, increased engagement in reading, better prosocial development, and college and career readiness."*
>
> *—Taun Wright*

Julie: We often hear the argument that "well, my school just isn't diverse." Although your school may not be racially diverse, your students still hold a range of personal identity markers, including family structures, gender expression, disabilities, mental health status, orientations, and body types. Our schools—and our student populations—*are* beautifully and wonderfully diverse. Library collections at every level—elementary, middle, and high school—need to reflect your student population. Our collections also need to reflect our diverse country and world. As educators, we are committed to our students being part of a global reality.

Even if—*especially* if—your school population is mostly or solely White, you should build a collection that is racially diverse and not restrict students to a single lens. All students deserve great stories—and if you're not including BIPOC authors and characters—then you're not truly giving your students all the possible great stories.

Stephanie: White and female tends to be the authoritative voice that defines diversity within the library profession. It is a place of privilege for White librarians to not have to recognize the importance of and the need for diverse collections. It is also a privilege to not see diversity beyond skin color. The work that is being done to break down the barriers of this authoritative narrative is a step in the right direction.

Julie: Building a diverse collection takes intentionality and effort because major U.S. publishers' offerings do *not* represent the diversity of our youth. According to the 2018 statistics compiled by the Cooperative Children's Book Center, there were more children's and young adult books published featuring animals and inanimate objects than there were books featuring Native, Latinx, Black, and Asian/Pacific Islander characters *combined* (Huyck and Dahlen 2019). This is why it's so important to dive deeper into your collection development and foreground #OwnVoices titles and counterstories.

Commitment to Diversity

Diversity in resources, however, is not enough. We must commit to pairing a diverse, inclusive collection with diversity within our own internal work, mind-set, and pedagogical frameworks—equity, antiracism, and decolonization. As we unpack how a commitment to this work drives our library programs, we use these touch points: starting at the beginning, the myth of neutrality, strategies for building an inclusive collection, and the importance of inclusive programming.

Starting at the Beginning

Julie: To meaningfully curate texts that center diverse voices, it's helpful to use a variety of lenses and frameworks for collection development, including:

- Mirrors, Windows, and Sliding Glass Doors—Rudine Sims Bishop
- #OwnVoices—Corinne Duyvis
- Danger of a Single Story—Chimamanda Adichie
- Plot-Driven Adventures across Identities—Malinda Lo
- Black Joy—Many Writers!

Mirrors, Windows, and Sliding Glass Doors. This is the gold standard for critically looking at representation in our collections and was pioneered by Rudine Sims Bishop. (Whenever referencing this idea always cite Sims Bishop. Education has a history of erasing the contributions of BIPOC scholars, particularly Black female scholars—interrupt that practice!) Her analogy is a foundational understanding for the importance of diverse books for all students.

"Books are sometimes windows, offering views of worlds that may be real or imagined, familiar or strange. These windows are also sliding glass doors, and readers have only to walk through in imagination to become part of whatever world has been created and recreated by the author. When lighting conditions are just right, however, a window can also be a mirror. Literature transforms human experience and reflects it back to us, and in that reflection, we can see our own lives and experiences as part of the larger human experience. Reading, then, becomes a means of self-affirmation, and readers often seek their mirrors in books" (Bishop 1990, ix).

Self-affirmation happens when our students have books that serve as mirrors—mirrors of themselves, of their experiences, and of their families and communities. For far too long, students from marginalized communities have been overexposed to window books and been deprived of the power of looking at literature through a mirror. Purchase more books where your students from marginalized communities can see themselves! And purchase books that show all readers the rich tapestry of human experience.

Prioritizing #OwnVoices Books. Disability in Kid Lit cofounder and author Corinne Duyvis coined this hashtag on Twitter in 2015 as a way to identify and recommend youth literature where the author and protagonist share a marginalized identity. Simply put, *who* gets to tell stories—who controls the narrative—matters! When authors have cultural and lived experiences that match those of their characters, the work has nuance and substance that can be seen and felt by the reader—especially when the reader also shares the same identity. Make #OwnVoices a purchasing priority and clearly state in your collection management plan that these books are sought out first.

Negating the Single Story. In her seminal TED Talk "The Danger of a Single Story," Chimamanda Adichie shares her own first experiences with reading to show how "impressionable and vulnerable we are in the face of a story, particularly as children" (Adichie 2009). Adichie connects insights on reading, writing, power, stereotypes, and story, and the joy of reading books that reflect the reader. Conversely, if we are only offering stories that tell a single narrative—often negative—about a community, culture, or country, we are perpetuating dangerous stereotypes. As librarians, we can push back against the single story by searching out multiple perspectives and authors to represent a wide range of cultures, communities, and realities.

> *"Stories matter. Many stories matter. Stories have been used to dispossess and to misalign, but stories can also be used to empower and to humanize."*
>
> —*Chimamanda Adichie*

Plot-Driven Adventures. Young adult (YA) author Malinda Lo stated in a book review that although "we need books that talk about race and racism, we also need books where characters of color can simply have the same kind of plot-driven adventures that white characters have all the time" (Lo 2015). This charge can truly be used as another framework for collecting—not only in terms of race and ethnicity—but for all kinds of diversity.

For example, while we need LGBTQIA+ stories that focus on coming out, we also need LGBTQIA+ characters who are having plot-driven adventures, across genres. Disabled and neurodiverse characters, Muslim characters, and characters with a range of body types likewise need to be shown having plot-driven adventures. And, it is our job as school librarians to seek out these stories and purchase them for our collections!

Include Joy. There is a problematic focus on narratives of pain for marginalized communities, especially for Black communities. This can be true for libraries and throughout the school, particularly for language arts and history class texts. We need to disrupt this practice! YA author Nic Stone tells us, "As we read all the race and racism books, we must also read books about Black people—especially Black children—just . . . living" (Stone 2020).

With three of my students—Cesar Falcon, Jose Gomez, and Jaida Morris—I (Julie) developed the #LibFive: Five Key Foundations for Building Inclusive Libraries:

- See Me! Listen to Me.
- Show Me on the Shelves and Walls—Read Those Books Yourself.
- Graphic Novels and Manga Are Not Extra.
- Show the Joy in Our Stories!
- Make the Library a Sorting-Free Zone.

For the fourth foundation—Show the Joy in Our Stories!—Jaida described how important it is to see books that reflect Black joy. Her previous school libraries centered books with Black stories solely around themes of struggle and pain. As part of her #LibFive action research, Jaida walked through our Mount Vernon Library, writing down things that she liked about the space. Her very first bullet point she wrote was *Black People Look Good*!

Use Jaida's wisdom. Reflect on your collection and space. Are your books that center Black stories concerned solely with slavery, civil rights struggles, and police brutality? Are your books that feature Latinx stories centered only on immigration? Are your books that center queer-identifying teens focused only on discrimination or bullying? Joy is an essential part of reading and library programs—and it is an essential part of our collections.

Myth of Neutral Library Collections

Nancy Jo: Libraries and librarians are not neutral. As school librarians, we have committed to the points outlined in the ALA Library Bill of Rights. Resources "should not be excluded because of the origin, background, or views of those contributing to their creation," and we "should provide materials and information presenting all points of view on current and historical issues" (ALA 2019). Like classroom teaching, serving as an effective school librarian is a political act. By offering youth a free, public education where they have access to information and all sides of issues, we equip them with the skills they need to navigate learning and to form opinions of their own. We train our students to recognize injustice through teaching history and reading literature. So, when we see injustice, we cannot shy away from it.

Stephanie: We can ask ourselves, who does neutrality benefit? Who is marginalized by neutrality? Neutrality in the library arena can be viewed as a scapegoat as it permits librarians to avoid promoting titles that aren't viewed as "safe" for students. *The Hate You Give* (THUG) by Angie Thomas is an example of a title that has been banned in some schools where *To Kill a Mockingbird* (TKAM) is considered a classic. This kind of "neutrality" allows TKAM to remain a classic while it marginalizes the voice of THUG.

Building Inclusive Collections

"Diversity is not praiseworthy, it is reality."

—*Malinda Lo*

Julie: Building an inclusive collection is—to put it lightly—an all-encompassing, never-ending endeavor. Successful curators of inclusive, diverse collections read widely, advocate for sufficient funding, stay abreast of reviews, and foreground following BIPOC, Queer, and Disabled authors and reviewers on social media. They listen to their students—actively collecting structured feedback via surveys and circulation data. They also observe students' reading habits and interests, and not only those students who are active library users. School librarians learn just as much—or more—about the new titles, subgenres, and formats we need to add to our collections by noticing who is *not* using our libraries.

Stephanie: It's vital that we invite classroom teacher and student input into collection building. Classroom teachers can often provide insight to resources students may need that librarians can curate. Inviting ourselves to teacher-planning sessions and Professional Learning Team (PLT) meetings gives librarians the opportunity to be visible in and supportive of the needs of our students.

Additionally, and most importantly, including student voice and choice in planning for inclusive and diverse collections is key. A diverse group of students at our school approached my library partner and me to help start a digital literary magazine as an outlet of expression during the COVID-19 pandemic. This magazine not only serves as an archive of students' thoughts during this moment in history, but it also allows for the library to establish and build on relationships with students. Relationships can help promote student input in the development and curation of collections that are inclusive and diverse.

Julie: Building an inclusive, diverse collection is going to look different at every school because every school's student population is unique. These elements, however, are common touchstones:

- **Learn about your students.** Begin each year with an engaging quick survey that teases out key information. Think of it as a macrolevel readers' advisory.
  - Don't only ask about books or reading!
  - Find out about your students' wide interests, including sports, music, games, anime, and social media influencers.

- Find out about their talents—writing, drawing, music, sports, languages, STEM, speaking, and more.
- Use that information to identify books to add to your collection.
- If there are no books on a trending artist or topic, find articles and either curate a list of digital resources for independent reading or print out copies in advance to have on hand.

- **Use #OwnVoices review sources and a wide social media and virtual PLT network to stay aware of new titles.** For this to be meaningful, your networks cannot be homogenous.

  - Fifty percent (at a minimum) of the people we follow professionally on social media should be BIPOC educators, librarians, writers, academics, and creatives.
  - Ensure you are following people that self-identify from communities representing a range of gender identities, orientations, religions, disabilities, and countries of origin.

NOTE: Please do not ask people you follow on social media to explain things to you. Read and listen to what is already out there. When you share their work, cite the creator behind it. All the steps above are not one-time-only events. To sustain a current, relevant, living collection, these steps need to be ongoing.

Building Inclusive Programming

Julie: Although nonnegotiable and a foundation for all that we do, simply having a diverse collection is incomplete. Books that reflect our students and our world need to be intentionally and seamlessly displayed, promoted, personally read, and incorporated into the classroom curriculum. Beyond our promotion and inclusion of our diverse collection, there is more that we must do to build inclusive programming.

Use culturally relevant and sustaining teaching methods for both your library instruction and classroom curriculum, coteaching, and collaboration. The pioneer of culturally relevant pedagogy (CRP), Gloria Ladson-Billings introduced this term to describe effective teaching. Based on her research, she identified three tenets of CRP—academic success; positive racial, ethnic, and cultural identity development; and student exploration of social justice issues (Ladson-Billings 1995). These tenets focus on asset-based teaching as opposed to deficit-oriented methods. With an asset-based approach, educators look at the identities, languages, and experiences of our students and their families as elements to be valued, celebrated, and as opportunities for learning—not as barriers.

Work to diversify the canon in your school. Diverse library programming cannot exist in a school where classroom texts for language arts are overwhelmingly White. As literacy leaders in our schools, we need to support classroom teachers in choosing #OwnVoices texts that represent the diversity of our world. #DisruptTexts created by Tricia Ebarvia, Lorena Germán, Kimberly Parker, and Julia Torres is a key resource in this effort. #DisruptTexts is committed to challenging "the traditional, White-centered canon to create a more inclusive, representative, and equitable language arts curriculum that our students deserve" (2020).

Diverse Collections and Programming Require Courage

Have courage to fully and lovingly represent and advocate for our students' whole selves in our library collections and programming and throughout the learning community. Have courage to push for meaningful #OwnVoices representation in the content curriculum. Have courage to do the necessary and continual internal work to understand our own place and part in oppressive systems. This necessary courage is not extra—it is our job as school librarians. We must do the necessary accompanying equity work, realistically assess our collections with audits, and tackle inclusive collection strategies that move beyond the foundations.

Equity Work

Nancy Jo: As a White cisgender woman, I want to stress the importance of White identity work. It takes courage to look at ourselves through the lens of race and see how Whiteness is centered in our collections, curriculum, and library programming. If you are a White person reading this, think about the world around you and the world in which you grew up surrounded by Whiteness—in books, media, and your community. An excellent place to start identity work is through the modules of Project READY (2018; ready.web.unc.edu).

Initial Diversity Audits

Nancy Jo: The starting point for evaluating your collection is to determine the racial and ethnic breakdown of your school. These data should be readily available online from your school or district. For example, the demographics of my school—Reedy High School—in 2019 were:

- Hispanic: 11.4 percent
- American Indian/Alaskan Native: 0.69 percent
- Asian: 24.35 percent
- Black: 6.21 percent
- Native Hawaiian/Pacific Islander: 0.05 percent

- White: 53.58 percent
- Two or more racial/ethnic identities: 3.98 percent

Our high school opened in 2015. I didn't choose our opening library collection. I have been purchasing books for my library for five years. We have approximately 2,000 students a year on our campus, give or take a few hundred each year.

In 2019, our student library aides and I worked on a diversity audit of our fiction collection. Two students who were as invested in this process as I am helped me create the Google form that we used to catalog identity markers of race, income, body type, immigration status, and LGBTQ+ status of the titles' main characters. We also collected information on the race of the author.

Doing a diversity audit is about taking inventory and determining what's in the library collection. It also helps us as school librarians see what areas need to be further developed. Prior to conducting this diversity audit, I was operating under the assumption that I was building an inclusive collection. Now my collection development practices are driven by concrete data.

We scanned 2,158 fiction books in our print collection, and this is what we found:

- Ninety percent or 1,937 books had a White author.
- Sixty-three percent or 1,369 books were written by a woman.
- Eighty-two percent or 1,771 books had a White main character or assumed White main character.

Our collection doesn't even come close to representing our student population. As a result of these data, I am aggressively purchasing #OwnVoices books. I am also using this audit to help me weed. My next steps include:

- Weeding inaccurate or outdated books.
- Auditing titles with diverse characters for authenticity, negative stereotypes, or struggle scenarios.
- Adding healthy representation of all identities that affirms our students' experiences and helps people outside marginalized groups question and challenge harmful stereotypes.

Ongoing Collection Development

Julie: All of these activities should be done on an ongoing basis through an equity and diversity lens. I'm currently in my sixth year at my present middle school, and I've gutted and rebuilt the collection during that time to reflect both our students and the larger world, foregrounding BIPOC writers.

As a result of this work, over 85 percent of our fiction collection features characters who are BIPOC, identify as Queer, and/or carry another "diverse" identity maker [such as country of origin, religion, or disability]. So, how do I continue to improve my collection? Several ways are through maintenance, genrefication granularity, and looking beyond fiction.

Maintenance. As librarians, we know that yearly turnover of our collections is inevitable and necessary. Books get lost, or, as I like to think of it— they find a *new home*. New books are published. Some titles need to be weeded. Django Paris has said, "Think of your syllabus as an act of resistance; something to be posted in the streets, handed out at rallies" (Paris 2018). We can apply this idea to our book orders. When ordering new books and maintaining an exemplary diverse collection, would you be proud to hand out your order list as a tool of antiracism, or as a protest against oppression? Do the books we weed show we are eliminating books with harmful stereotypes or tropes steeped in racism or homophobia?

Also, we must guard against "soft censorship" where librarians refrain from collecting titles—often those centering LGBTQIA+ stories—because they are afraid of future challenges from families or other school stakeholders. Soft censorship might seem harmless, but it is a toxic practice that prevents vulnerable youth from seeing themselves meaningfully represented in their libraries. We can be ready for challenges by proactively building support in our schools and strengthening our collection management plans. Help yourself prepare by reading AASL's toolkit and guide: *Defending Intellectual Freedom: LGBTQ+ Materials in School Libraries* (AASL 2018). As youth librarian and YA author Alex London says: "It's a fight worth having . . . lives are on the line" (Yorio 2020).

Genrefication Granularity. Like many librarians, I've genrefied our fiction collection. Based on students' interests and input, I chose these genres: realistic fiction, humor, historical fiction, fantasy, science fiction, romance, animals, horror, and mystery. Focusing on specific genres helps me test how well I'm building an inclusive collection across and through genres and sub-genres. In other words, our romance and horror sections should ideally have as many #OwnVoices books as our realistic fiction and historical fiction sections. This is still an area of growth for me, and improving the #OwnVoices content of our horror and humor sections is specifically referenced in my most recent collection management plan.

Looking beyond Fiction. Fiction is obviously not the only section in our libraries. Our nonfiction section should also be combed through with an eye toward weeding books that tell—and sell—only a single story or are filled with toxic stereotypes and historical untruths. New titles must be prioritized, foregrounding books that provide counterstories and specifically challenge the Whiteness in historical narratives. In addition to nonfiction, assess and strengthen your graphic novel section to seek out a diverse, wide range of stories across genres within the format.

Nessa

Every single one of the librarians in our district is a White woman. We know this is prevalent in our profession, but it's still important to say. When a librarian comes to me with a question about deepening their ability to collect diverse resources, I say, "Let's start with identity work."

"You can't create a diverse collection unless you're willing to ask yourself some hard questions. There is no checklist."

—*Nessa*

Think Deeply

After engaging honestly in identity work, I would suggest they look over the collection again. Look for more #OwnVoices titles and specific #OwnVoices that are not only tragedy based. Then, turn to your school population. Give students choice! Give the kids some money to spend on books. What do they want to purchase? You want their thinking to be visible as to why they are gravitating toward certain authors and books. Then, after that? Make it sustainable. We make it sustainable with the kids, and then they will have expectations for the kind of collection and library that they want and know to expect—one that reflects them.

Look local. Look to your own state and community and the history there. Being in Oklahoma, I wanted to explore the Tulsa Race Massacre with students. The two often-used recently written youth books that deal with this history were both authored by White women; it's frustrating that so many schools are using these texts without question. As a profession, we should come together and help find, support, or demand from publishers a Black author to tell this story. I'm so excited at the news that Carole Boston Weatherford and Floyd Cooper have created a picture book to explore the Tulsa Race Massacre with youth (Carolrhoda Books 2021).

Think Widely

Think widely when considering diverse resources—what conversations are you having? For example, last year, when I served as a high school librarian, we organized monthly family meetings to discuss topics. One of our most powerful discussions looked at which schools around us did and did not celebrate Martin Luther King's birthday. Our school was unique in that we had it off—and we discovered that the Black families in our district had advocated for the school's recognition of MLK Day. This was important for us to recognize as a school community and as a library.

In addition to local in terms of state or community, look local in your own school! I was a high school librarian in a small town, and I discovered all of the school's artifacts, including yearbooks and newspapers. During the process of safely archiving them, students got involved and we looked at our school history critically. For example, we could tell when our school had integrated. Students developed research questions based on what they noticed and wondered. Students discovered—from analyzing past yearbooks—our school had Native and Latinx students in the 1930s, but not in later years. What happened? Through interviewing local families, we discovered that there had been a Black school—Excelsior Academy—associated with our current school, but we didn't have any of their materials. None of it was saved. We wanted to find it! Currently, there is a historian who is trying to rebuild this textual history and get materials from students' descendants—from attics, basements—to fill in this missing history. My students connected deeply to this project.

So, thinking diversely could live out very locally for you in your own school and community. Look at archived history from your town and school. What's missing? Who is missing? Not just in your fiction collection, but in your local history!

Think Critically

Across the board for digital resources through an equity lens, it's always about access. Just thinking about making our digital resources effective, let's look at what is compatible with what we already have. Think low floor, high ceiling—easy to use, easy to access with a lot of capability. Sometimes more is just more.

From attending tech conferences and then literacy conferences, I've found there is a very different feeling in terms of antiracism and antibias operating at these conferences. With tech, I've started looking more and more at the booth. I've started looking more at who is calling me. Who are tech companies picking for their sponsors or their influencers? I pay attention to that. When I assess digital resources, I look at the faces. I've started e-mailing companies with comments like "I really like your laser, but all the kids in your ads are White." Their response to my comment is an important consideration. Ultimately, I want a great product, but I want to get that great product from a company that is not steeped in racism. I'm not looking for token actions, but meaningful efforts. I'm looking at who are in positions of power at edtech companies.

Nessa is a district-level educational technology integration specialist for a public school district in the Southwest. A former school librarian, she is the district-level advocate for her district's school librarians.

Gabriel Graña

I've been in my library for six years. As the years have progressed, I've seen more self-selected, self-formed study groups, organic clubs of students of color who just want to come in and celebrate their interests. That's what I've been aiming for, and I'm so glad to get there with our library space!

Representation Is a Verb

Librarians new to antiracist work must understand why it's important that their collections reflect not only the students they mostly see in their spaces, but everybody's story. Think about how the world is bigger than just the students right there in front of you, and also fully realize that the students who are right there in front of you have multiple stories themselves, stories that need to be represented in your collection.

Talk to the kids! See what your students like and focus in on your students of color. I had a group of seventh-grade students last year that would come in as a group with similar interests. I started purchasing books specifically for them and their interests, knowing that this specific collection development would connect with other students, too. It's a way to authentically build out our collections tied to student interest. Also, it's so simple, but having a place where students can request specific titles or genres or subjects is so valuable—whether it's a physical box or something digital—or ideally, both. I take these suggestions and then when I get the titles, I put them on display with "Here's What You Asked For!" signage.

We've always got to think about the voices that aren't being heard. That's powerful. Talk to the students that are *not* dropping in. Ask them: "What's going to bring you to the library? What can I do?" I had a student who wasn't checking out books, even when his class came, and I just asked him point blank: "Bro, what am I going to put in your hands?" He replied with "maybe . . . something on cars?" And, that's all it took. He checked out what we had and helped me find some newer options. If you want your library collection to reflect not only your students, but their interests, you have to bring them into the process. It also requires that we be flexible in how we gather that feedback.

It's so important that we seek not just a book with a Latinx main character telling, let's say, a Mexican or Cuban story. Instead, identify a fantasy novel with a Cuban protagonist where his Cubanness is a part of him, but not the main focus of the story and where that Cubanness is still told authentically. Think of diversity in *that* sense. It is so much bigger than just having books you can put up for Black History Month or Asian Pacific Heritage Month. Search out that intersectionality—for example, Kacen Callender's *King and the Dragonflies* (Scholastic 2020). It's not just a Black story or a Queer story, it's also a fantasy. Think of that level of diversity!

Stepping into a Larger World

Let's look at displays for example. Perhaps you're doing a display of science fiction titles—whatever your theme is—look at who is represented. Not just the characters, but the authors. Are there authors of color and authors from other marginalized groups? How deep is your representation? How genuine is the diversity? Do you have Native American sci-fi titles? Do you have a Latinx character in space written by a Latinx author with Latinx issues embedded in there? Doing this kind of digging is so important!

In following other librarians and libraries on social media, I get ideas for promoting the space and collection with students. This has been especially helpful while doing distance learning! With my librarian account on Instagram, @bibliograna, I started with #WhatchaReadingWednesday to booktalk specific titles and #FessUpFridayLibrary to highlight quirks with my own reading life. My goal for both is to go beyond promoting books to also promote the reading lifestyle and everything that accompanies it. I want to reach students who may not yet identify as readers. I have a space to talk about what I'm reading, and also about reading habits. I want to be honest and vulnerable about what it is to read. I'm authentic when I'm on Instagram and sharing videos. I don't script my material in advance—I'm just myself. Soon I'll be adding #FandomFridays, which will give me a chance to geek out about different fandoms with my students. We're also—my students, my colleagues, and I—going to start doing #30SecondBookTalks. I'll then share these out on multiple platforms—social media like Instagram, on the library website, and directly with students during virtual or in-person classes.

Gabriel (he/him/el), el bibliotecario Cubanito, has been the librarian at RD & Euzelle Smith Middle School for seven years. His collection development and programming are driven by student interests and requests. Follow him on social media @bibliograna to geek out with him about Star Wars, hip-hop, social justice, representation in media (especialmente LatinX), and, oh yeah, libraries.

Commitment: Ongoing and Far-Reaching

The work for us—all of us—is to continually do better with and for our students. In terms of diverse resources, this means curating a collection across a wide range of formats that actively reflects our students and the world across a beautifully wide range of identities. Our collection development includes more than the buying and maintaining of resources. If our collections are just sitting prettily on a shelf, that is a shallow effort on our part and not nearly enough for our students. We have to use and promote the fullness of our collections in a way that purposefully centers the identities of communities that have been marginalized—through booktalks, literature circles, community reads, displays, and reader's advisory.

Once we've done that? Then, we move to the next step, because diversity of resources in our own spaces is just the beginning. We then take our knowledge and commitment—our purpose—and use it to transform the collections throughout the school, including classroom collections and the *books chosen as classroom texts*. For our students, seeing themselves in the library is not enough—they need to see their rich and whole selves in the curriculum and school community, too. We—you, personally and our school library profession as a whole—can help make this happen.

Reflection Questions

1. How has your own cultural context influenced the books you've read—both within school and personally? How has this shaped your collection development frameworks as a school librarian?

2. What steps can you take to disrupt the "single story" and one-sided narrative that is represented in much of children's and young people's literature?

3. What steps can you take to affirm diversity beyond the library and reflect on how you can influence stakeholders—and especially other educators—throughout your school?

References

Adichie, Chimamanda. 2009. "The Danger of a Single Story." Filmed July 2009 at *TEDGlobal*. Video, 18:34. Available at https://www.ted.com/talks /chimamanda_ngozi_adichie_the_danger_of_a_single_story?language=en. Accessed October 1, 2020.

American Association of School Librarians. 2018. "Defending Intellectual Freedom: LGBTQIA+ Materials in School Libraries." *American Association of School Librarians*. Available at https://standards.aasl.org/project/lgbtq. Accessed October 1, 2020.

American Library Association. 2019. "Library Bill of Rights." *American Library Association*. Available at http://www.ala.org/advocacy/intfreedom/library bill. Accessed October 1, 2020.

Bishop, Rudine Sims. 1990. "Mirrors, Windows, and Sliding Glass Doors." *Perspectives* 1(3): ix–xi.

Brown, Brené. 2018. *Dare to Lead. Brave Work. Tough Conversations. Whole Hearts.* Vermillion: London.

Callender, Kacen. 2020. *King and the Dragonflies.* New York: Scholastic.

Disrupttexts. 2020. "What Is #Disrupt Texts?" Available at https://disrupttexts .org/lets-get-to-work. Accessed October 1, 2020.

Huyck, David, and Sarah Park Dahlen. 2019. "Diversity in Children's Books 2018." *sarahpark.com* (blog). Created in consultation with Edith Campbell, Molly Beth Griffin, K. T. Horning, Debbie Reese, Ebony Elizabeth Thomas, and Madeline Tyner, with statistics compiled by the Cooperative Children's Book Center, School of Education, University of Wisconsin–Madison: http://ccbc.education.wisc.edu/books/pcstats.asp. Available at https://readingspark.wordpress.com/2019/06/19/picture-this-diversity-in -childrens-books-2018-infographic. Accessed October 1, 2020.

Ladson-Billings, Gloria. 1995. "But That's Just Good Teaching! The Case for Culturally Relevant Pedagogy." *Theory Into Practice* 34(3): 159–165.

Lo, Malinda. 2015. "Recommended Read: 'The Third Twin' by CJ Omololu." *Malinda Lo* (blog), February 24. Available at https://www.malindalo.com /blog/2015/02/recommended-read-the-third-twin-by-cj-omololu. Accessed October 1, 2020.

Paris, Django. 2018. "Think of Your Syllabus . . ." @django_paris Twitter post, August 9. Available at https://twitter.com/django_paris/status/10275909 48404875265. Accessed October 1, 2020.

Project READY. 2018. "Getting Started: Curriculum Guide." Available at http://ready .web.unc.edu/getting-started-curriculum-guide. Accessed October 1, 2020.

Stone, Nic. 2020. "Don't Just Read about Racism—Read Stories about Black People Living." *Cosmopolitan*, June 8. https://www.cosmopolitan.com /entertainment/books/a32770951/read-black-books-nic-stone. Accessed October 1, 2020.

We Need Diverse Books. n.d. "About WNDB." Available at https://diversebooks .org/about-wndb. Accessed October 1, 2020.

Weatherford, Carole Boston, and Floyd Cooper. 2021. *Unspeakable: The Tulsa Race Massacre.* Minneapolis, MN: Carolrhoda Books.

Yorio, Kara. 2020. "Not Quite Banned: Soft Censorship That Makes LGBTQIA+ Stories Disappear." *School Library Journal*, February 4. Available at https:// www.slj.com/?detailStory=not-quite-banned-soft-censorship-makes -LGBTQIA-stories-disappear-libraries. Accessed October 1, 2020.

CHAPTER 3

Inclusion

Meg Boisseau Allison and Peter Patrick Langella

> Inclusion means welcoming and affirming the voices of
> all library stakeholders in a way that shares power.

Radical

In a 2019 talk at TEDxStowe on "Radical Diversity," Kiah Morris, a former Vermont state representative and current movement politics director at Rights & Democracy Vermont, shared that she can "not rest easy over small changes or mediocrity."

> *"Understand that if we are to create a vision for what this diverse world looks like, it must be radical, or it will fail."*
>
> —Kiah Morris

Morris resigned from office in 2018 following a targeted hate campaign from a self-avowed White nationalist in Bennington, Vermont, and she is still seeking justice from the state's attorney general. Her vision and courage have inspired our commitment to inclusion in the school library. It must be radical, or it will fail. It must be intentional, or it will fail. It must be made through coalition building and collaboration, or it will fail.

Radical Inclusion

Radical inclusion means an absolute focus on policies and practices that "demonstrate an understanding of and commitment to inclusiveness and respect for diversity in the learning community" (AASL 2018, 76). Radical inclusion means that libraries are not neutral or apolitical spaces. Radical inclusion means understanding that the library is a reflection of the greater community and dominant culture, and therefore its priorities must ebb and flow to maintain steadfast equity of access and opportunity.

Educator Teresa Bunner (2017) worked with students in North Carolina to create the Student Six initiative to ensure that we "create learning spaces in which every student feels acknowledged, valued, and included as equal members of the community" (41). To enhance our focus on inclusiveness and diversity, we need to ask ourselves related questions and take decisive action on the answers:

- How do we know whether students feel welcomed and visible in the library space?
- Is our signage clear and in various languages?
- How about our resources? Do our curricula meet our inclusive goals?
- What community connections can we build to help normalize and honor nondominant cultures and intersectional identities in our programming?
- How can we turn our library into a hub for courageous conversations?
- Are there opportunities for explicitly addressing race in the library?
- In what ways do our school libraries reinforce inequities and injustices by choosing what we remain silent about?

Libraries are not neutral or apolitical spaces. Chris Bourg, director of libraries at Massachusetts Institute of Technology says, "The very notion that shared, consolidated community resources ought to exist is not a neutral proposition. A library as an institution represents a decision about how a community spends its resources, and those decisions are not neutral" (ALA 2018).

This notion of libraries as neutral may stem from language in the American Library Association's Library Bill of Rights (2019), which centers equal access for all voices and ideologies. At first glance, it may be easy to interpret this document as applying only to public libraries, but ALA's "Interpretations of the Library Bill of Rights" says that "the principles of the Library Bill of Rights apply equally to all libraries, including school libraries" (2014).

We don't agree. For example, we'd never allow exclusionary or hate-based groups to use our libraries as planning hubs. All speech cannot be equal in school libraries, especially if that speech aims to marginalize, dehumanize, or harm students from historically oppressed backgrounds.

> *"Let us stop debating about how to be neutral and start arguing about how to use our power as a profession to shape a better society."*
>
> —R. David Lankes

Because the library is a reflection of the greater community and dominant culture, and because we want to be part of that better society, opportunity and accessibility gaps that exist must be accounted for, audited, and disrupted. Gloria Ladsen-Billings, author and University of Wisconsin education professor, says, "A culturally relevant teacher is someone who understands that we're operating in a fundamentally inequitable system. . . . The idea is not to get more people at the top of an unfair pyramid; the idea is to say the pyramid is the wrong structure. How can we really create a circle, if you will, that includes everybody?" (cited in Thomas 2019).

School librarians are uniquely situated to make an impact in this regard because we have access to learners beyond the conventional classroom. We have a sphere of influence and a considerable amount of control over that space. Paul Gorski (2020), founder and lead equity specialist at the Equity Literacy Institute, explains further: "More than cultural competence or diversity awareness, equity literacy prepares us to recognize even the subtlest forms of bias, inequity, and oppression related to race, class, gender identity and expression, sexual orientation, (dis)ability, language, religion, immigration status, and other factors."

Identities and Intersections

Before we get too far into exploring radical inclusion and the way we put it into practice in our libraries, it's important to own our intersectional identities. Learning for Justice writes that "being an effective ally requires significant self-reflection and a strong sense of self-identity. Any educator can become an ally, but the journey might look different depending on one's identity, experience, and familiarity with issues of power and privilege" (2018).

Through identity map protocols from organizations like Seed the Way (https://seedtheway.com) and the Dialogue Arts Project (https://dialoguearts project.com), we have begun the work to decentralize our dominant identity markers, recognizing the fluidity of them based on context. Building more inclusive spaces and libraries is a necessary, early step toward radical inclusion.

Understanding intersectionality, then, is to recognize "the social, economic and political ways in which identity-based systems of oppression and privilege connect, overlap, and influence one another" (Bell 2016). As White, cis-gendered, able-bodied, middle-income librarians, we acknowledge our identities have baked-in advantages in a society that privileges these identities. Peter's male identity adds another huge layer of privilege to the equation, and it creates a perpendicular intersection with Meg, who identifies as female. We understand that we have more social capital to spend in the struggle to dismantle systemic racism, sexism, anti-Semitism, xenophobia, transphobia, gender binaries, heterosexism, able-normativism, or other language and actions in our libraries, schools, and other spheres of influence.

We acknowledge that we both work in well-funded public schools that enjoy broad community support. Our library programs are each staffed by two certified teacher-librarians and one full-time assistant. We acknowledge that many librarians from historically marginalized communities, and/or who work in libraries without adequate funding, encounter injustices in their library policies, practices, and communities that impact them disproportionately and traumatically.

The Work

A group of Danish public librarians have begun referring to some of their newer, redesigned (both in terms of space and purpose) libraries as the "living room of the city . . . focused on human needs" (Morehart 2016). This can be accomplished through both our curricula and our relationships and partnerships with our learning community.

> *"At the individual level, when we embrace equity literacy we learn to become a threat to the existence of inequity and an active cultivator of equity in our spheres of influence."*
>
> —*Paul Gorski*

Social Justice through Compassionate Action

In *How to Be an Antiracist* (2019), Ibram X. Kendi says, "Knowledge is only power if knowledge is put to the struggle for power. . . . Changing minds is not activism. An activist produces power and policy change, not mental change" (209).

This is striking for librarians to think about at first encounter; at least it was for us, two privileged librarians in Vermont. Since 1990, when Rudine Sims Bishop's essay "Mirrors, Windows, and Sliding Glass Doors" was published, librarians have had a framework for reflection and empathy building to apply around literature instruction and appreciation. Others have updated it since then, like Uma Krishnaswami's "Why Stop at Windows and Mirrors? Children's Book Prisms" (2019) and Debbie Reese's (2018) "curtain" metaphor for Indigenous stories.

The idea that reading can build empathy is supported by brain science (Berns et al. 2013). But, in order to learn together and share power, "we need to grow our students and colleagues from ignorance and apathy all the way through sympathy and empathy to get to a place of compassionate action and future-building" (Allison and Langella 2020).

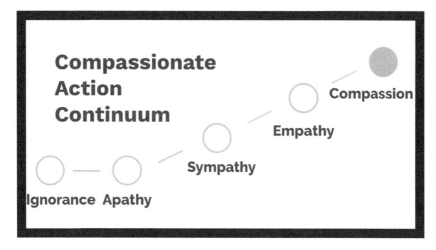

Figure 3.1 Compassionate action.

We modeled this framework on the Intercultural Development Inventory (https://idiinventory.com) as a way to help us understand Kendi's call for action. Peter first used the Compassionate Action Continuum as a unit and writing assignment, respectively, in elective classes he taught. He then worked with colleagues Emily Rinkema and Stan Williams, coauthors of *The Standards-Based Classroom: Making Learning the Goal* (2018), and a group of students to design a class called "Social Justice Think Tank."

The course has four distinct parts based on the Social Justice Standards: The Learning for Justice Anti-Bias Framework (2016): Identity, Diversity, Justice, and Action. As an example, after engaging in extensive identity work and reading *How It Went Down* by Kekla Magoon (Henry Holt 2014), a book about the shooting of an unarmed Black teenager by a White vigilante, "one student zeroed in on the idea that guns kill people. . . . This then led her to think about the school's policy that no guns are allowed on campus, and the contradictory presence of an armed School Resource Officer (SRO)" (Allison and Langella 2020). She then planned to get the school board to remove the officer and hire more counseling staff or, at least, remove the gun from the officer if the officer remained. The campaign has not met either of its goals at the time of this writing due to the COVID-19 school closure and other factors. However, the student has displayed immense growth on the learning continuum, especially by attempting to use her learning to disrupt inequity and power hierarchies and asking for policies and practices more aligned with justice.

"The school library facilitates opportunities to experience diverse ideas by promoting the use of high-quality and high-interest literature in formats that reflect the diverse developmental, cultural, social, and linguistic needs of all learners and their communities" (AASL 2018, 77). Our commitment to this standard must be "more than books on the shelves" (Langella 2019). Peter worked for years and years to help the educators in his school disrupt and update their reading lists and classroom practices, but, other than a few teachers and a few lessons, the impact wasn't systemic until his colibrarian Christina Deeley brought Project LIT Community (PLC) to their school.

PLC is "a grassroots literacy movement empowering readers and leaders in hundreds of schools and communities around the world" (@ProjectLITComm 2016). And even though it was created as a curated book club, Christina and Peter were able to build partnerships that turned PLC into a part of the curriculum for ninth-grade humanities classes.

During the first year, Peter's groups read *Long Way Down* by Jason Reynolds (Atheneum 2017) and *The 57 Bus* by Dashka Slater (Farrar Straus Giroux 2017), respectively. Students were dissecting their own social conditioning and possible misconceptions by "evaluating a variety of perspectives . . . [and] engaging in informed conversation" (AASL 2018, 76). For example, *The 57 Bus* is about a teen named Sasha in Oakland, California, who identifies as agender and uses they/them pronouns. Sasha is badly burned on the bus one afternoon on the way home from school when another teenager lights Sasha's skirt on fire.

Peter and the students spent a lot of time discussing gender and sexuality—and the hate and discrimination directed at people who don't identify as heterosexual or along the male/female binary—at a time when the Trump administration was "considering an interpretation of Title IX . . . that 'would define sex as either male or female, unchangeable, and determined by the genitals that a person is born with'" (Delpit 2019, xvii). One student immediately spoke up about the existence of intersex people. A couple of members of the group had never heard this term (or didn't understand it), so it was important to be able to contextualize and grow in a small learning community.

In the late spring of 2020, gender identity was in the headlines because people were speaking out against author J. K. Rowling's antitransgender and anti-nonbinary tweets that went "against all advice given by professional health care associations" (Radcliffe 2020). Peter and *The 57 Bus* book group were able to reconvene to process together, and to collectively figure out what it means to be a better ally to—and advocate for—the LGBTQIA+ community. When you make the decision to disrupt and decolonize the canon, and when you use that journey as a way to build a learning community, that's radical inclusion. Students will be much more likely to continue to move beyond understanding and empathy in favor of compassionate action.

Prides and Prejudices

In order to continue to teach directly with students, school librarians with flexible schedules need to radically transform pedagogies and models of embedded librarianship, a framework that positions school librarians where the learners are. It creates conditions where librarians become true coteaching partners. It is radical as it frees up the school librarian to be positional to the learning, not the circulation desk. It provides students with proximity not just to library resources, but to a librarian as well.

At the highest scale of this model of coteaching, what we see emerge is an iteration of radical inclusion—creating pockets of transformational learning that extend the boundaries for students and colleagues alike.

Enter high school English teacher, Jenn Ingersoll.

Jenn reached out to Meg with a radical idea. She needed a co-conspirator to chart an alternative course in the traditional AP World Authors curriculum, and disrupt the notion of the canon as a whole.

The movement to #DisruptTexts (2020) was created by four educators and school librarians: Tricia Ebarvia, Lorena German, Kimberly Parker, and Julia Torres. Their mission to support the "grassroots effort *by* teachers *for* teachers to challenge the traditional canon in order to create a more inclusive, representative, and equitable language arts curriculum that our students deserve" calls on educators to be radically inclusive. Jenn believed they could create a case to disrupt the canon with Ibi Zoboi's *Pride* (Balzer + Bray 2018), a contemporary remix of Jane Austen's *Pride and Prejudice*.

Meg and Jenn have cotaught the unit two times, the first time nearly tripping over themselves as they discovered alongside their students the brilliance of Zoboi's text as a culturally relevant remixing of class and gender expectations. The narrative stands on the shoulders of literary giants as Zuri, a contemporary of Elizabeth Bennett, writes spoken word poetry, which Zoboi uses to break up the narrative flow. This text within a text provides readers with an intimate lens into the structural inequities of Zuri's neighborhood, including gentrification and redlining, code switching and urban divestment, and the complications of upward mobility and race. Unpacking gentrification was rendered relevant through explorations of change in their students' Vermont villages, as rural general stores transform into gourmet shops and artisanal bakeries, and by contextualizing insider and outsider perspectives of place.

Heroine Zuri Benetiz is firmly in the #DisruptTexts resistance, fighting back against the Anglo-Saxon canon by the very reality of her identity alone. To invite her into the AP classroom was a radical invitation. By setting *Pride* within Bushwick, many students found a sliding door into a world of stoops and bodegas, daps and block parties. The coteachers created guideposts for these cultural markers, as most of their students had never been to Brooklyn. For a few students of color, they found a much-needed mirror, all too often missing in the formal curriculum. They found a heroine in Zuri Benetiz, who looked like them and sounded like them, even if the only common denominator was that she wasn't White.

As a culturally relevant text, *Pride* beats with radiant joy and infectious energy. The Haitian and Dominican symbolism and spirituality Zoboi weaves throughout her story reveals that the African diaspora is never far, linking this text firmly into the World Authors lineage. Zuri, as a manifestation of the Ochun Orisha, is a water goddess tracing back to the Yoruba of Nigeria. Zuri's self-actualization that "if oceans are the wounds of the world, then I am the interconnecting umbilical cord with deep love flowing" solidifies *Pride*'s rightful place within the AP World Authors curriculum, complementing if not outright supplanting *Pride and Prejudice.*

If texts are being chosen to disrupt the canon, so too should traditional assessments. Within *Pride,* spoken word is a disruption to traditional poetry presented in anthologies students encounter as AP students. Likewise, teaching spoken word provides a divergent assessment of themes of race and class, and the prides and prejudices embedded deep within. Some students are uncomfortable with new formats, yet others thrive in finding their voices in nontraditional forms. Too often, student papers are written for an audience of one, the teacher, robbing them of an authentic audience. Shifting the assessment from an essay to a spoken word performance gave students chances to "demonstrate empathy and equity in knowledge building" and to "reflect on their own place" within the larger community (AASL 2018, 76). For one student, Addie Hannan (2019), this assignment revealed unexplored stories of identity and belonging:

> I can't remember the last time there was a conversation about race
> that didn't get weird.
> I always feel eyes upon me,
> I am seen as all-knowing,
> an expert.
> I get it, the color of my skin stands out against my mostly white class.
> But still, I have lived here for almost my entire life,
> I am a Vermonter through and through,
> Please don't ask me where I'm really from,
> Because I already told you,
> And you know what else?
> My parents are white,
> And English is my native tongue.

An essay about Jane Austen, after delving into nineteenth-century England, wouldn't have opened up Addie to her own extraordinary truths, nor given her teachers and classmates a sliding door into her experience, nor provided her with a platform to spit her truth.

The Courage to Build Liberatory Third Spaces

If our vision is to cocreate a third space with a diverse coalition of stakeholders, we can operate as an inclusive ally, advocate, activist, and/or agitator, depending on the situation. We might become, for our students, the embodiment of an antibias barometer: a resource for students to go to, individually and collectively, when they see something in their community and need to report it.

We have both created anonymous reporting portals for our communities through our library websites to ensure that students can feel safe when they stand up to hate, and most students respect and appreciate that. Mica Pollock (2017) goes even further: "As educators, it's our job to denounce hate and intimidation where we work, to make sure students feel safe to learn." As we've said, libraries are not neutral spaces. We believe harm has been done in the name of free speech in our library spaces and have come to understand, very deeply and through experience, that while almost any topic is up for educational discussion in the library, one's humanity is not up for debate.

To center radical inclusion, when librarians denounce hate and hateful acts, we are ever mindful of our role as educators to intervene. Learning for Justice's "Speak Up at School" guide (2019) urges us to "Speak up against every biased remark—every time, in the moment, without exception" (48). When we see a need, we step up, ready with information to help students make sense of their world. We saw this with the rising interest in antiracism books in the aftermath of the murders of George Floyd, Breonna Taylor, Tony McDade, Ahmaud Arbery, and others in the spring of 2020, and the massive, sustained protests that took to the streets all over the United States.

But many school librarians stop there. Not only that, many readers stop there, too. Author Jason Reynolds said, "I'm grateful that people are working to seek out information to help them better understand what's happening in our country, and I hope it's not a knee-jerk reaction due to shame and guilt and not wanting to be on the outside. I hope people understand that this . . . is the beginning of a journey of a lifetime" (cited in Harris 2020). The pivot toward radical inclusion is to take the act of curating and reading books that address inequities, or that celebrate Black history, Indigenous history, and so on, one step further, toward amplifying these texts in the creation and curation of radically inclusive spaces. Spaces in our libraries to hold courageous conversations that then become incubators for compassionate action.

There, students can refine their voices and are empowered to speak. They tap into their innate courage and integrity, and we can help amplify them. There, they are visible in their full humanity and diversity as creators of their own liberation.

It's important to note that cocreating space is in contrast to "giving voice."

> *"The idea of 'giving' students voice, especially when it refers to students*
> *of color only serves to reify the dynamic of paternalism that renders*
> *Black and Brown students voiceless until some salvific external force*
> *gifts them the privilege to speak."*
>
> —Jamila Lyiscott

In "Why Social Justice in the Library? | Outreach + Inreach," Margo Gustina and Eli Guinnee question whether libraries fall short by usually offering equal access, in lieu of "active equitable access that focuses on empowering the less powerful and amplifying the voices of the unheard" (2017). School libraries have a role to disrupt the fallacy of providing equal access by centering historically marginalized voices in our schools. In doing so, we can help amplify the inequities and injustices they encounter, ensuring their voices reach important stakeholders in our learning communities.

VIGNETTE: HATE MANIFESTS

Meg Boisseau Allison

On June 4, 2018, the Black Lives Matter flag was raised at my school. Students of color advocated courageously, sharing that raising the flag would mean "they have a place in school . . . that they matter." The student body's reaction was wide ranging. Although largely supportive, many White students felt conflicted. Some expressed support of racial equality but not the method of protest. Others stepped up to learn about allyship and decentering Whiteness in Seeking Social Justice, a group colleague Amy Koenigbauer and I cofounded with our students. There was a small but vocal openly intolerant student contingent.

I felt our school needed more time for workshops and dialogues, unknowingly perpetuating a racial equity detour identified by Paul Gorski as "pacing for privilege." As I struggled at planning meetings, the faculty advisor for our students of color, Krista Dy, shared that raising the flag was to serve as a catalyst for change, not merely as an exclamation point.

In retrospect, I have greater awareness of Martin Luther King Jr.'s teachings from "Letter from a Birmingham Jail" (1963), in which he wrote of the White moderate as someone who impedes racial justice. "I agree with you in the goal you seek, but I can't agree with your methods of direct action; who paternalistically feels he can set the timetable for another man's freedom." However, I am left to wonder if a long-range educational campaign might have prevented hate from bubbling up to the surface at our school. I am left to wonder if it could have prevented another flag raising that very same day at our school.

That of the Confederate flag.

As Noah Witke-Mele, a student in Seeking Social Justice, was walking into school that morning, he saw a shocking sight. Flying out of the back of a school bus were two flags, one a Blue Lives Matter flag, the other the Confederate battle flag. Noah snapped a picture, and with that act, changed the course of conversations in our school for the next eighteen months. The unequivocal display of the Confederate flag on this particular day, of all days, was none other than a display of racial intimidation.

Just as the library hosted conversations facilitated by students of color to speak of racism at school, the library needed to be the place to host conversations about hate. This is radical inclusion: to make space for even the most abhorrent ideas, to shine a light on them, and get uncomfortable. This work aligns with the AASL standards (2018), enabling students to exhibit empathy and tolerance, and "demonstrate an understanding of and commitment to inclusiveness and respect for diversity" by co-constructing "a learning environment that fosters the sharing of a wide range of viewpoints and ideas" to give "learners opportunities to engage in informed conversation and active debate" (76).

When cofounding Seeking Social Justice, we weren't initially concerned with policy change. Creating a space to address rising incidents of ignorance and hate was our goal. Concerns echoed among colleagues about the purported neutrality of the library. Shouldn't a school library be the very place within a school where a student can wrestle with any number of ideas and viewpoints without one having more weight than another? If, by speaking out against the Confederate flag, or in favor of gun control, or LGBTQIA+ rights, and creating spaces in the library for dialogue, was I compromising the intellectual freedom of our students? Was the library becoming embroiled in partisanship?

Emphatically, no.

Neutrality in the library speaks loud and clear of apathy at best, and complicity at worse. If the library is the physical and metaphorical heart of a school, what good does it do to be indifferent? Silence serves the oppressors, and in an educational setting, it's imperative for the school librarian to be an agitator for disrupting that silence and providing opportunities to speak out.

Students used the library to plan for faculty meetings, advisory activities, and opportunities for their peers to dialogue about hate symbols in our school. Over 50 percent of students replied in a student-created survey that they were interested in learning more about the Confederate flag's historical and contemporary contexts. What we quickly discovered was the different interpretations of the flag. For nearly all students who reported "not feeling safe" when seeing the flag, it was because the flag represented racism and hate. Not one student who supported or displayed the flag said it was because they were racist; rather, their support fell under an umbrella including pride in southern heritage, rural values, patriotism, or rebellion.

After our first hate ban proposal was rejected by our school administration, we were later asked to reopen the discussion. On the first day of school, a student of color shared that he did not feel safe at his new school. One of his classmates was wearing a Confederate flag hat.

We got back to work.

We tackled hate right off the bat and invited the mother of the student charging the complaint to a new evening dialogue series called "Rolling Up Our Sleeves." These conversations used protocols, including chalk talks and shared reflections. What we heard loud and clear was a sense of urgency to enact a ban on the Confederate flag. We noticed a small but emboldened group of students wearing the flag to school. We invited these students in so they could be heard but also listen to the flag's impact.

We crafted a policy proposal and hosted multiple readings of it, "engaging in informed conversation and active debate" (AASL 2018, 76). Students spoke at events, presented at board meetings, and facilitated conversations with faculty. Finally, in February 2020, our board adopted a policy change to eliminate all hate symbols, including the Confederate flag, in noneducational contexts.

Conversations in the library had a school-wide impact, led to policy change, and kickstarted initiatives to interrogate curricula. Conversations brave enough to disrupt a status quo that prefers "a negative peace which is the absence of tension to a positive peace which is the presence of justice" (King 1963). This is radical inclusion.

Meg (she/her) is a teacher librarian in Vermont. Meg earned a bachelor's in sociology and anthropology from Colgate University, and a master's in curriculum and instruction from the University of Vermont. She is a past recipient of a Global Teacher Fellowship, a Vermont Outstanding Teacher award, and is a corecipient of the Vermont Outstanding School Librarian Award with Peter Langella.

Vignette: "I Agree with the Students"

Peter Patrick Langella

It was early 2019, and a leadership meeting for the student Racial Alliance Committee (RAC) that I advise was about to begin in the library. We were in the middle of deliberations to convince the school board to agree to raise the Black Lives Matter flag and sanction associated educational programming.

The library was packed with students transitioning between blocks.

"Is that what I think it is?" said a student, gaping at one of our whiteboard tables.

It was. The n-word, written in a swooping script, next to a swastika. I reached for the eraser and began scrubbing the table.

"You should've taken a picture," the student said.

But I wouldn't have had enough time because the student leaders of RAC arrived at my side just as I finished. The students didn't need to experience the visual.

I asked the student who discovered the scene if they'd be willing to talk with the administration, and they said yes. I then faced the RAC leaders and delivered the devastating and unsurprising news that our school wasn't any different. We had students with vitriol in their minds and hearts, and at least one or some of them weren't afraid to show it.

After meeting with the students, I tried to find our principal. He was unavailable, so I gave the news to one of the assistants. He was disappointed that I didn't preserve the evidence or take pictures. He said he'd reach out to the corroborating student, and the school would begin an investigation. He made sure to let me know that these things are rarely solved. Just the semester before, there had been a series of n-words found in a couple of student bathrooms, and several swastikas had been discovered carved into classroom desks. N-words had been directed at Black students on buses. A Black student had been pushed to the ground in the hall and called "monkey." These were all on top of the incidents I already knew about through discussions as the RAC advisor.

Nothing came of it.

I left the office in a daze. How had the larger community never heard about these acts of racism and anti-Semitism in our school? And, if we didn't know about them, how could we reflect and learn and grow?

In RAC meetings in the months prior to this, we'd been talking about how most people associated with the school didn't think we needed to have a more robust conversation about race and racism because our student body was over 90 percent White. The student leaders and I had actively been trying to help the administration understand that everyone is impacted by systems of racism, oppression, and White supremacy. But the needle hadn't moved much. It was clear the administration did not want to make racial equity a larger focus of curricula or professional development, even though they knew for certain it wasn't an abstract concept that only existed somewhere else. Hate was in the building, and they weren't including anyone in a process to try to stop it.

I drove home that day reflecting on the moments before the student and I came across the table. At least a dozen students had been there, mostly popular eleventh and twelfth graders, and no one said anything. I wondered if they'd all been involved in the act, if many had been oblivious, if we really had that many ignorant and apathetic bystanders at our school, or some combination along that continuum? Compassionate action was clearly *not* in effect. This reflection led me to wonder what radical inclusion could look like for my school and community. What choice could I make that would honor the lives of my students, firmly take a side, and give the most people the best opportunity for—and access to—justice?

I had to file a police report.

I had to use my immense privilege and social capital, especially those broad avenues of White, cismale-ness that I own—the identities that afford me the right to engage in an extraordinary amount of open conflict with superiors—to make sure that the administration couldn't "solve" this internally.

I didn't make that decision lightly. Just like they are in the rest of the country, I knew that many members of the community were disproportionately targeted by police in Vermont (Seguino and Brooks 2019). People from historically marginalized and oppressed backgrounds, particularly Black people, were some of the very folks the messages of hate were meant to directly harm.

My principal was deeply disappointed that I didn't involve him in that decision. The conversations that followed with him, the police, and the students were challenging. The principal almost canceled everything RAC had been working toward. It all came to a climax one afternoon in the library. The principal and the students got into a heated argument about race, racism, justice, and the school's commitment, or lack thereof, to grow. Everyone looked to me when the exchange reached an impasse. The tension was pulsing through the space. I looked every person there in the eye before saying five words: "I agree with the students."

It created a proverbial line in the threading of the stained, faded carpet of the library that might exist forever.

Then, the formal police investigation into the hate at our school helped the community speak. We learned about the harm those words and symbols cause. We learned about their links to long-standing campaigns of discrimination and violence—not from a book or a movie or some far off voice, but from our neighbors, who came into the library and shared their stories and experiences, face to face. The administration had to own their apathy, intentional or not. It was time to listen, learn, and grow.

I've been called an agitator. I've been called a radical. And I know I've helped our students shift the school's priorities so they are more in line with the future we're seeking together.

Peter (he/him) is a librarian and social justice advisor at a high school in Vermont. He earned a master of fine arts in writing for children and young adults from Vermont College of Fine Arts. Peter also works as a school library instructor at the University of Vermont, and an English instructor at Northern Vermont University.

Merging Radical Inclusion with Compassionate Action

In that same talk on "Radical Diversity," Kiah Morris ended with a quote that has been attributed to Lila Watson and other Australian Aboriginal elders from the 1970s: "If you have come here to help me, you are wasting your time, but if you have come because your liberation is wrapped up with mine, then let us work together."

Youth activist Hazel Edwards agrees. In conversation with Learning for Justice, speaking specifically about transgender rights, Hazel said, "If youth, and specifically trans youth, are not given seats at the table to be able to bring their perspectives and their experiences and the ways that they could be best supported, then the policy or the legislation or whatever the rule is will not adequately support [them]" (cited in Lindberg 2017).

"Nothing about us, without us, is for us."

—Hazel Edwards

This is radical inclusion. This is compassionate action.

Radical inclusion in school libraries means first doing important identity work in order to recognize how our privilege (or lack thereof, in some cases) relates to our social conditioning, environments, practices, and spheres of influence. Radical inclusion means an absolute focus on policies and practices that are made *with* students and *by* students to be inclusive of their intersectional identities, in all of the ways we've described, and more that we hope we can still learn. Radical inclusion not only means that libraries are not neutral or apolitical spaces, but that they are liberatory spaces with librarians who are active agents striving to side with students against isms and phobias and other forms of bias, discrimination, marginalization, and oppression. Radical inclusion means understanding that the library is a reflection of the greater community and dominant culture, and therefore it is inherently inequitable. Access and opportunity gaps must be recognized, audited, and dismantled in order to build a more just future.

Whether it's the mundane or the profound—the books we order, the classes we teach, the programs we run, or the conversations we facilitate with members of our learning community—we must make sure that everyone knows what the school library stands for: collective liberation, compassionate action, and radical inclusion.

Reflection Questions

1. In what ways do you reinforce inequities and injustices by choosing what you remain silent about?

2. How can you cocreate a sense of belonging for all students, across all intersectional identity groups? What is your response to a student(s) who says and does things that break your established social contract of radical inclusion and unconditional acceptance?

3. A vision statement is a collective expression of a community's highest aspirations. What could a vision statement say for your school library if it was cocreated to center collective liberation, compassionate action, and radical inclusion?

References

Allison, Meg Boisseau, and Peter Langella. 2020. "Compassionate Action in School Libraries: Using Books and Brave Conversations to Harness Student Voice and Move beyond Empathy." *School Library Connection*, April.

American Association of School Librarians. 2018. *National School Library Standards for Learners, School Librarians, and School Libraries*. Chicago: ALA.

American Library Association. 2014. "Interpretations of the Library Bill of Rights." *American Library Association*. Available at http://www.ala.org/advocacy /intfreedom/librarybill/interpretations. Accessed October 1, 2020.

American Library Association. 2018. "Are Libraries Neutral?" *American Libraries*. Available at https://americanlibrariesmagazine.org/2018/06/01/are-libraries -neutral. Accessed October 1, 2020.

American Library Association. 2019. "Library Bill of Rights." *American Library Association*. Available at http://www.ala.org/advocacy/intfreedom/librarybill. Accessed October 1, 2020.

Bell, Monita K. 2016. "Teaching at the Intersections." *Learning for Justice*, Summer. Available at https://www.learningforjustice.org/magazine/summer-2016 /teaching-at-the-intersections. Accessed February 16, 2021.

Berns, Gregory S., Kristina Blaine, Michael J. Prietula, and Brandon E. Pye. 2013. "Short- and Long-Term Effects of a Novel on Connectivity in the Brain." *Brain Connectivity* 3(6): 590–600. doi:10.1089/brain.2013.0166. Accessed October 1, 2020.

Bishop, Rudine Sims. 1990. "Mirrors, Windows, and Sliding Glass Doors." *Perspectives* 6(3): ix–xi.

Bunner, Teresa. 2017. "When We Listen: Using Student Voices to Design Culturally Responsive and Just Schools." *Knowledge Quest* 45(3): 38–45.

Delpit, Lisa, ed. 2019. *Teaching When the World Is on Fire: Classroom Conversation in Challenging Times*. New York: New Press.

Disrupttexts. 2020. "What Is #Disrupt Texts?" Available at https://disrupttexts .org/lets-get-to-work. Accessed October 1, 2020.

Gorski, Paul, ed. 2020. "Equity Literacy for Educators: Definition and Abilities." *EdChange*. Available at http://www.edchange.org/handouts/Equity-Literacy -Intro-Abilities.pdf. Accessed October 1, 2020.

Gustina, Margo, and Eli Guinnee. 2017. "Why Social Justice in the Library? | Outreach + Inreach." *Library Journal*. Available at https://www.library journal.com/?detailStory=why-social-justice-in-the-library-outreach -inreach. Accessed October 1, 2020.

Hannan, Addie. 2019. "Untitled." Poetry assignment, U-32 High School.

Harris, Elizabeth A. 2020. "People Are Marching against Racism. They're Also Reading about It." *New York Times*, June 5. Available at https://www .nytimes.com/2020/06/05/books/antiracism-books-race-racism.html. Accessed October 1, 2020.

Kendi, Ibram X. 2019. *How to Be an Antiracist*. London: One World.

King, Martin Luther, Jr. 1963. "Letter from a Birmingham Jail." Available at https://www.africa.upenn.edu/Articles_Gen/Letter_Birmingham.html. Accessed October 1, 2020.

Krishnaswami, Uma. 2019. "Why Stop at Windows and Mirrors? Children's Book Prisms." *The Horn Book*, January 17. Available at https://www.hbook .com/?detailStory=why-stop-at-windows-and-mirrors-childrens-book -prisms. Accessed October 1, 2020.

Langella, Peter. 2019. "Diversity and Inclusion in Libraries: More Than Books on the Shelves." *Knowledge Quest* (blog), May 13. Available at https://knowledge quest.aasl.org/diversity-and-inclusion-in-libraries-more-than-books-on-the -shelves. Accessed October 1, 2020.

Learning for Justice. 2016. "Social Justice Standards: The Teaching Tolerance Anti-Bias Framework." *Southern Poverty Law Center*. Available at https:// www.learningforjustice.org/sites/default/files/2020-09/TT-Social-Justice -Standards-Anti-bias-framework-2020.pdf. Accessed February 16, 2021.

Learning for Justice. 2018. "How to Be an Ally." *Learning for Justice*, Spring. Available at https://www.learningforjustice.org/magazine/spring-2018/how-to -be-an-ally. Accessed February 16, 2021.

Learning for Justice. 2019. "Speak Up at School: How to Respond to Everyday Prejudice, Bias and Stereotypes." *Learning for Justice*. Available at https:// www.learningforjustice.org/magazine/publications/speak-up-at-school. Accessed February 16, 2021.

Lindberg, Maya. 2017. "Nothing about Us without Us Is for Us." *Learning for Justice*, Fall. Available at https://www.learningforjustice.org/magazine/fall -2017/nothing-about-us-without-us-is-for-us. Accessed February 16, 2021.

Magoon, Kekla. 2014. *How It Went Down*. New York: Henry Holt.

McMahon, Martin. 2019. "U-32's Confederate Flag Debate." *U-32 Chronicle*, June 13. Available at https://u32chronicle.com/2019/06/13/u-32s-confederate-flag -debate-part-2. Accessed October 1, 2020.

Morehart, Phil. 2016. "Moving beyond the 'Third Place.'" *American Libraries*, August 17. Available at https://americanlibrariesmagazine.org/blogs/the -scoop/library-design-moving-beyond-third-place. Accessed October 1, 2020.

Morris, Kiah. 2019. "Three Tools for Anyone Serious about Radical Diversity | Kiah Morris | TEDxStowe." *YouTube* (video). Posted by *TEDx Talks*, May 31,

2019. Available at https://www.youtube.com/watch?v=UPfdAX—6ME. Accessed October 1, 2020.

Morris, Kiah. 2020. "Black Lives Matter Hour of Unity." Virtual speech, U-32 Middle & High School, East Montpelier, VT, June 4.

Pollock, Mica. 2017. "Standing Up against Hate." *Learning for Justice* 56 (Summer). Available at https://www.learningforjustice.org/magazine/summer-2017 /standing-up-against-hate. Accessed February 16, 2021.

ProjectLitComm. 2016. "Bio." @ProjectLitComm. Available at https://twitter.com /ProjectLITComm. Accessed October 1, 2020.

Radcliffe, Daniel. 2020. "Daniel Radcliffe Responds to J. K. Rowling's Tweets on Gender Identity." *The Trevor Project* (blog), June 8. Available at https://www .thetrevorproject.org/2020/06/08/daniel-radcliffe-responds-to-j-k-rowlings -tweets-on-gender-identity. Accessed October 1, 2020.

Reese, Debbie. 2018. "Critical Indigenous Literacies: Selecting and Using Children's Books about Indigenous Peoples." *Language Arts* 95(6): 389–393.

Reynolds, Jason. 2017. *Long Way Down.* New York: Atheneum.

Rinkema, Emily, and Stan Williams. 2018. *The Standards-Based Classroom: Make Learning the Goal.* Thousand Oaks, CA: Corwin.

Seguino, Stephanie, and Nancy Brooks. 2019. "Data Needs to Track Racial Dispari- ties in the Vermont Criminal Justice System." University of Vermont and Cornell University, September 10. Available at https://stephanieseguino .weebly.com/uploads/2/3/2/7/23270372/recommendations_on_revisions _to_race_data_collection_statute_20_v_8.22__v7.pdf. Accessed Octo- ber 1, 2020.

Slater, Dashka. 2017. *The 57 Bus.* New York: Farrar, Straus and Giroux.

Thomas, P. L. 2019. "Unsweet Tea: On Tokenism, Whiteness, and the Promise of Culturally Relevant Teaching." *Radical Eyes for Equity* (blog), October 1. Available at https://radicalscholarship.wordpress.com/2019/10/01/unsweet -tea-on-tokenism-whiteness-and-the-promise-of-culturally-relevant -teaching. Accessed October 1, 2020.

Zoboi, Ibi. 2018. *Pride.* New York: Balzer + Bray.

CHAPTER 4

Intellectual Freedom

Suzanne Sannwald and Dan McDowell

Intellectual freedom, including access and choices, privacy and confidentiality, is the right of all library stakeholders.

Passion: Exploring Our Passion for Intellectual Freedom

As colleagues working within the same district, we have cowritten this chapter on intellectual freedom, each contributing perspectives strengthened by our respective expertise and experiences. Suzanne is a practicing high school librarian, and Dan, a previous classroom teacher and director of Instructional Technology Services, now serves as director of Learning and Innovation. As we explore our passion, commitment, and courage related to intellectual freedom, we address various aspects of this core value of school librarianship. Starting with passion, we share what has inspired each of us to examine intellectual freedom in new ways:

- Expanding Our View of Intellectual Freedom by Suzanne Sannwald
- Preparing Students as Members of a Democratic Society by Dan McDowell

Expanding Our View of Intellectual Freedom

When first approached about writing this chapter on intellectual freedom, my immediate response was that I, Suzanne, was probably not qualified to address the topic since I have never faced a book challenge in my work as a school librarian. My gut response was not necessarily surprising. After all, one of the most visible intellectual freedom campaigns that occurs every year is Banned Books Week, hosted by ALA's Office for Intellectual Freedom, OIF (2020b). My reaction, however, was admittedly and embarrassingly far too narrow in scope. Although advocating against book banning falls squarely within the realm of intellectual freedom, intellectual freedom is a core value of librarianship that we must weave into our everyday practice, not just in the event of a book challenge. Fortunately, on further reflection, I know intellectual freedom is indeed a value that informs my work on a regular basis; I just have not always internally labeled it in this way in the past. Hopefully, this chapter will also help refresh, reframe, or reaffirm your understanding of intellectual freedom so that you, too, will see the various ways it shows up in your practice, demanding both your commitment and courage.

As described in the ALA's *Intellectual Freedom Manual*, intellectual freedom "is used in the library profession primarily to mean the right of every individual to both seek and receive information from all points of view without restriction" (Jones 2015, 3). Book challenges clearly conflict with an individual's rights to seek and receive information; however, what are other ways that intellectual freedom shows up in our school libraries? My next thought was about web-filtering policies, a natural transfer of looking at restrictions to information within digital realms. It was at this point that I thought of inviting Dan McDowell to coauthor since he previously served as the director of Instructional Technology Services for our district and was instrumental in crafting technology use policies for students.

As I continue to read and reflect on intellectual freedom, I grow increasingly passionate about even more expansive possibilities for school librarians to defend and promote intellectual freedom within our learning communities. Ensuring students' rights to seek and receive information is intricately tied to equitable access; it relies on it. Having unrestricted access to information from all points of view requires that there is diversity in resources and programming and inclusion of all voices. Intellectual freedom is not a standalone core value, but one that intricately and inseparably intersects with equity, diversity, and inclusion. Intellectual freedom is not a value that we should only claim when a resource is formally challenged. Intellectual freedom is an ever-relevant value that school librarians must intentionally embrace to identify perhaps less immediately visible, but still insidious, breaches that exist and persist when left unaddressed.

Preparing Students as Members of a Democratic Society

Intellectual freedom issues have never been more critical. I, Dan, am writing this chapter from home in the midst of the COVID-19 pandemic, which has highlighted important concerns as we navigate distance learning. We are also experiencing the ups and downs of a presidential election cycle, controversies swirling around the pandemic, and the Black Lives Matter movement. It is essential that our students have access to the web and social media to stay informed and participate.

Our district opened up the web several years ago. Before I moved to the district office and became the director of Instructional Technology in 2013, our district had strict web-filtering policies. As a social science teacher, I would often identify a website at home as a key resource for one of my classes and discover the next day as my students were trying to access it that it was blocked. In most cases, I was able to complete a request form and have the individual article or website unblocked. My students, of course, did not have the same access to have items whitelisted. As a result, their research was always hampered by an algorithm run by a filtering company that was overly protective for a high school environment.

One of the first challenges I took on as I moved to the district office was to reframe our educational community's view of the Internet as a vast resource. Working with educators and administrators, we took our technology acceptable use policy and turned it into a responsible use policy. Instead of listing all possible infractions, we highlighted the power of open access to information in an innovative environment. With that cultural shift in place, we opened up access to Flickr, YouTube, and so much more. Although there was a lot of concern expressed initially, our students have embraced the trust we put in them.

Schools today have a responsibility to provide that access and facilitate discussions around information literacy. A democratic society requires open access to information, and that must start in our schools. As a school librarian, you can play an integral role in helping secure these access and educational rights for students by embracing your commitment to intellectual freedom and acting with courage.

Commitment: Understanding and Embracing Intellectual Freedom as a Core Value

Having established our passion for intellectual freedom—how we need to view it expansively and with as much urgency as ever—we revisit the ALA definition: "the right of every individual to both seek and receive information from all points of view without restriction" (Jones 2015, 3). With this basic explanation in mind, we may read headlines about school library stakeholders challenging book titles or blocking web content, but if they are not happening in our schools, we may feel absolved from feeling like we have work to do. It may also be difficult to know what exactly a comprehensive commitment to intellectual freedom entails since it requires translating an abstract concept into everyday practices. With this in mind, a good place to start may simply involve learning the basics of and becoming familiar with key resources related to intellectual freedom.

Legal Precedence

At its core, intellectual freedom is rooted in the First Amendment of the U.S. Constitution. Many may think of the First Amendment in short as being about "freedom of speech" or "freedom of the press." However, Supreme Court decisions have established that the First Amendment also secures our right to receive information since receiving information is a corollary to the right to speak. Although there are numerous related rulings to explore, two Supreme Court decisions are frequently cited when it comes to school libraries and intellectual freedom. *Tinker v. Des Moines Independent Community School District* held that students do not "shed their constitutional rights to freedom of speech or expression at the schoolhouse gate" (Fortas 1969). *Board of Education, Island Trees Union Free District No. 26 v. Pico* rejected the removal of books from a school library since students are included as beneficiaries of "the right to receive ideas is a necessary predicate to the recipient's meaningful exercise of his own rights of speech, press, and political freedom" (Brennan 1982).

> *"While [school librarians] may not consider themselves 'defenders of democracy,' they frequently act in that capacity when they protect minors' rights to read and receive information under the First Amendment and case law."*
>
> —Helen R. Adams

Professional Guidance

Looking at professional standards, you will find that ALA provides a great deal of guidance, which while not enforceable provides more tangible guideposts for our work. To start, intellectual freedom is embedded in ALA's Code of Ethics. Out of the code's eight total principles, the second and third directly relate to intellectual freedom:

- **Principle 2.** We uphold the principles of intellectual freedom and resist all efforts to censor library resources.
- **Principle 3.** We protect each library user's right to privacy and confidentiality with respect to information sought or received and resources consulted, borrowed, acquired, or transmitted (ALA 2020a).

Principle 2 directly calls out intellectual freedom, whereas Principle 3 relates to privacy and confidentiality. This is no mistake! Protecting the privacy and confidentiality of library users also falls under the umbrella of intellectual freedom. "Privacy is essential to free inquiry because it enables library users to select, access, and use information without fear of embarrassment, judgement, surveillance, punishment, or ostracism" (Magi 2015, 171). Meanwhile, confidentiality, which Adams refers to as privacy's "twin concept" (2013, 164), requires librar staff to not divulge users' personal information to others.

Additional key documents from ALA to explore related to intellectual freedom include the Freedom to Read statement, which opens asserting, "The freedom to read is essential to our democracy," and ends with, "the suppression of ideas is fatal to a democratic society. Freedom itself is a dangerous way of life, but it is ours" (ALA 2004). This is some revolutionary language, and it is backed up by ALA's very own Library Bill of Rights, which notably applies to children with "age" specifically called out as nonexcluding and extends beyond reading to listening, viewing, and other modes of taking in information and ideas.

The American Library Association affirms that all libraries are forums for information and ideas, and that the following basic policies should guide their services.

I.   Books and other library resources should be provided for the interest, information, and enlightenment of all people of the community the library serves. Materials should not be excluded because of the origin, age, background, or views of those contributing to their creation.

II.   Libraries should provide materials and information presenting all points of view on current and historical issues. Materials should not be proscribed or removed because of partisan or doctrinal disapproval.

III. Libraries should challenge censorship in the fulfillment of their responsibility to provide information and enlightenment.

IV.   Libraries should cooperate with all persons and groups concerned with resisting abridgment of free expression and free access to ideas.

V.   A person's right to use a library should not be denied or abridged because of origin, age, background, or views.

VI.   Libraries which make exhibit spaces and meeting rooms available to the public they serve should make such facilities available on an equitable basis, regardless of the beliefs or affiliations of individuals or groups requesting their use.

VII. All people, regardless of origin, age, background, or views, possess a right to privacy and confidentiality in their library use. Libraries should advocate for, educate about, and protect people's privacy, safeguarding all library use data, including personally identifiable information.

Source: http://www.ala.org/advocacy/intfreedom/librarybill. Reprinted with permission: American Library Association Office of Intellectual Freedom

Figure 4.1 Library Bill of Rights.

Intellectual freedom is broadly about seeking and receiving information, privacy and confidentiality, and democracy. But, what does this look like in your day-to-day school library life? Some of the most helpful guidance we've found regarding tangible applications of intellectual freedom are official "interpretations" of the Library Bill of Rights, which address topics including:

- Access to library resources and services for minors.
- Access to resources and services in the school library.
- Minors and Internet activity.
- Economic barriers to information access.
- Services to persons with disabilities.
- Challenged resources.
- Diversity in collection development.
- Evaluating library collections.
- Labeling and rating systems.
- Privacy.

Library Bill of Rights interpretations may be read for free online, but the *Intellectual Freedom Manual* collects them all and includes additional discussion specific to different types of libraries, including school libraries. The manual is published by the ALA's OIF, the group that not only hosts Banned Books Week, Banned Websites Day, and Choose Privacy Week, but also provides support all year round in the form of resources, training, and consultation should you ever face a book challenge. They are the office that you report incidences of censorship to and that annually releases lists of most frequently challenged titles and other statistics.

Why School Libraries?

Looking at OIF's data regarding challenges, it becomes crystal clear why school librarians in particular must become informed about and advocate for intellectual freedom. In 2019, nine of the ten most challenged books were ones written for children or teens, and a strong argument could be made to include *The Handmaid's Tale* as a tenth (ALA 2020d). Many of these challenges are happening in our schools, with 69 percent of challenges from 1990 to 2010 recorded as originating in schools and school libraries (Fletcher-Spear 2014, 13). And, perhaps most concerning, challenges disproportionately affect materials written by and featuring some of our most marginalized populations, including LGBTQIA+ and people of color (Oltmann 2017).

As a school librarian, you may be one of the few people at a school site who is aware and informed enough to defend intellectual freedom. Furthermore, school library collections offer a unique "point of voluntary access to information and ideas" (Magi 2015, 120), affording greater latitude when it comes to empowering intellectual freedom than with classroom curriculum. As articulated in *Right to Read Defense Committee v. School Committee of the City of Chelsea* (1978), "The library is 'a mighty resource in the marketplace of ideas.' There a student can literally explore the unknown, and discover areas of interest and thought not covered by the prescribed curriculum." With the library's distinctive position in our schools, we school librarians must approach our work with an expansive mind-set that maximizes this powerful potential.

> *"Intellectual freedom, as a principle and a mind-set, creates space*
> *for many voices to be present."*
>
> —*Shannon Oltmann*

As you will see in the following vignette, a mind-set for intellectual freedom includes securing students' choices when accessing resources. It is also fostering their agency in the learning process through the types of experiences that educators develop and facilitate. Maintaining a commitment to intellectual freedom is thus multifaceted, not only focusing on resources, but on our whole pedagogical approach.

VIGNETTE: ADVOCATING FOR STUDENT CHOICE AND AUTHENTIC INQUIRY

Shelly Buchanan

Working in a K–8 school, I engage in a wide array of conversations related to student choice with independent reading. On the one hand, I have the occasional parent (or sometimes classroom teacher) approach me with concerns about their child's book selections and whether they are appropriately challenging. They may want their child to move beyond picture books or early chapter books or fantasy novels (commonly considered fluff reading), and want me to direct their child to more advanced books. I try to be tender and empathetic while assuring parents that their child will get "there," but that our young reader may want, or even need, to read *Stellaluna* a hundred times or read the entirety of *The Keeper of the Lost Cities* series multiple times before moving on to something else, and that is okay, too. When a parent asks, "Why does my kid keep checking out *Nate the Great* over and over and over again?" I explain that it's likely because they really need to. I try to protect children's choices for themselves. The important thing is that we are supporting our eager readers!

On the flip side, there will be the kindergartener walking out library doors with a giant *Harry Potter* book that they can barely carry and cannot read, and I explain that is okay, too, that this is aspirational reading. I encourage parents to allow their reader to check out *Harry Potter*, even if it is just sitting on the child's bedside table, because maybe it is their reading north star of the moment, and so let's support that dream. Of course, in most cases, the student will return the book a few days later. They might say, "Shelly, I'm not really ready for this yet," or "This book is a little boring for me," and I tell them that is all right, that the book will be here when they are ready and interested.

In my mind, the true success of a child's independent reading experience depends largely on personal choice. Therefore, if I encounter a parent or classroom teacher who remains uncertain about their student's book selections, my suggestion is for the student to check out additional books, titles that the adult recommends and ones the child wants to read as well. Often, I mention Stephen Krashen's deep research on the power and effectiveness of free voluntary reading on a child's academic and personal reading development, and most adults appear heartened by this news. A child's book selection does not need to be an either/or compromise but can be a yes-and opportunity instead. These are the types of conversations that I have with adults, but most commonly I engage in conversations directly with students about their reading experiences and tastes in books.

With students, I drill down on recent favorites and try to discern what elements of titles most engage the reader, and we go from there. I can never resist adding on one or two potential outliers that just might appeal in case the reader is feeling extra adventurous and is willing to try something different than their usual picks. This is also when I end up having a conversation with students about what they want to read and what suits their maturity level. As an example, I have an eighth-grade student eager to explore more serious and complex themes. During one library visit, I gave her five or six book recommendations, including Laurie Halse Anderson's *Speak*. I shared teaser soundbites for each title, and when I detailed the rape trauma in *Speak*, she responded quite assuredly, "No, I'm not ready for that yet, maybe later." This self-reflective reader understood with certainty that she was not ready for that kind of story yet. By conducting in-depth readers' advisory interviews with students, I have found that overall readers do a really good job of self-monitoring and knowing for themselves what feels right and appropriate. Trusting students is my default setting, and it proves effective. I love having that kind of relationship with my readers, and I sense they trust my reading recommendations.

Honoring student choice in freely exploring ideas and information has also been a major point of advocacy for me with our school's focus on student inquiry. I was initially inspired by what Arbor School calls the Independent Project when my own children attended the school years ago. As a parent, I got to witness the excitement and energy of my children when they were let loose to engage in their own selected independent project work. I witnessed the power in allowing kids to make their own intellectual choices, and I firmly believe that every single child in the world deserves to chase their personal curiosity. By foregrounding regular opportunities like the Independent Project or other student-driven learning experiences, we educators could systematically support our youth in discovering and honing their individual and collective interests and passions. Promoting their intellectual freedom in this way generates agency, allowing for their dynamic and powerful growth and holding the capacity to create young people with motivation and confidence to make a difference in their communities.

I should note that when I think about and strategize for student independence and empowerment, at the same time I am keenly aware of the need for students to connect with and support one another. Just as readers' advisory in the library and classroom relies on in-depth conversation, I believe inquiry work and learning is also strengthened in community. At the beginning of the year, in one experiment with this, I suggested to a classroom teacher that eighth-grade students engaged in their year-long independent inquiry projects connect with peers through a cohort experience. In these cohorts, students blogged with each other about their research project experiences, brainstorming and troubleshooting together. They celebrated each other's successes and cheered one another through challenging moments. Students had the freedom to deeply explore a topic of personal interest and the freedom to share it with others through the cohort experience and also whole school sharing. Each student inquirer became the school-wide expert on their selected pursuit. This to me is intellectual freedom writ large.

Shelly teaches and directs the library program at Arbor School of Arts & Sciences near Portland, Oregon. Past professor and English teacher, Shelly has presented locally, nationally, and internationally on student-driven inquiry. She is active in the National Council of Teachers of English, the Oregon Association of School Librarians, and the AASL.

Courage: Reviewing Existing Practices, Engaging in Self-Reflection, and Making Changes for Intellectual Freedom

As reflected in Shelly's vignette, school librarians can readily demonstrate our commitment to intellectual freedom through tangible, everyday practices within our school communities. In this section, we consider how we can be courageous and take action to reflect on, reevaluate, and reform even more practices. Operations can become so routine and ingrained that they are often easy to accept as a given rather than as systematized choices. Although this section is not an exhaustive list of areas to evaluate, it offers starting points for reflection and action related to selection and acquisitions, cataloging and circulation, curriculum and instruction, and laws, codes, and policies.

Selection and Acquisitions

The acquisition decisions that we make have the potential to either widen or limit the intellectual freedom of students. Do I avoid buying titles because I anticipate negative reactions from parents, administration, or the community? Do I not purchase materials because they conflict with my personal beliefs and values? If a book is age appropriate and not harmful to minors, and we avoid selecting it out of fear, then we are self-censoring, sometimes also referred to as soft-censoring.

Whelan (2009) refers to self-censorship as "a dirty secret that no one in the profession wants to talk about or admit practicing." But self-censorship is not a clear-cut issue. Determining age appropriateness can be an ambiguous task with a single title being recommended for different age ranges by various book reviewers, not to mention natural variations that exist in the development and experiences of children. Furthermore, even in 2020, we see bills such as the Parental Oversight of Public Libraries Act threatening to impose financial penalties and legal charges against librarians based on community challenges to materials and programming decisions (Diaz 2020). Having fear is understandable and legitimate.

Still, while adults may certainly have good intentions in wanting to protect students when determining what is appropriate or not, author Jarrett J. Krosoczka reminds us, "There are difficult truths in our books because there are difficult truths in children's lives" (2018). The very information that we might not allow students to access may in fact be part of their lived realities.

> *"You won't ever make a difference if you don't step out of the box. . . . Who knows? That very book that you thought was inappropriate may be the one that turns a child in the direction that he needs to be going or that gives a child quiet hope about a situation."*
>
> —Pat Scales

Cataloging and Circulation

The decisions that librarians make about cataloging and the physical arrangement of our collections are generally driven by wanting to make information as accessible to users as possible. Our intentions are most often positive, and yet examining them with intellectual freedom in mind may shed light on practices that are in fact limiting or harmful in ways that we do not intend. For instance, in a Future Ready Librarians Facebook group thread, a user asked, "Is it okay to put a sticker that says LGBT on the books to help me and the kids locate them easily?" Some replied that they do this or put books in a separate section so that students may find them easily, and yet others pointed out potential privacy and safety issues that may arise in doing so, suggesting instead to provide book lists and cataloging tags that allow students to locate materials more discreetly. With LGBTQIA+ books making up the majority OIF's Top Ten Most Challenged Books list for 2019 (ALA 2020c, 14), school librarians must become particularly informed on how to support intellectual freedom in this area. One helpful resource to consult is AASL's guide *Defending Intellectual Freedom: LGBTQ+ Materials in School Libraries* (AASL 2018a).

Along the lines of how we choose to label books, Coe Booth challenged, "It seems that any book with an African-American character on the cover is quickly being labeled street lit, regardless of the subject matter or setting of the book" (quoted in Whelan 2009), while books with White characters in urban settings are not. *Are we segregating the books on our shelves?* And, even if we are not separating books based on their characters or content, are we doing so in other ways such as labeling and organizing books by reading level? If we only allow students to check out books at a set level, we are in fact restricting their ability to choose information. If we organize books by levels and require students to browse only those sections, we doubly infringe on their intellectual freedom by removing their rights to privacy (Adams 2013, 33–34).

Other practices to reflect on and address to best support intellectual freedom include the following:

- Providing resources to English language learners in their primary language
- Ensuring full access to the collection without restricted shelves or sections
- Choosing with intention what information to highlight in library displays, web resources, and programming
- Identifying potential economic barriers to information such as with overdue fine policies and inequitable access to technology
- Implementing accommodations to facilitate access to information in library spaces online and in-person for persons with disabilities or specific instructional needs
- Respecting student privacy to browse collections without scrutiny or judgment

- Protecting student confidentiality with library circulation records such as not including title information on fine notices

Curriculum and Instruction

Unlike other types of librarians, school librarians have a primary responsibility as educators, and therefore it is important that we look at how we support intellectual freedom in terms of curriculum and instructional choices, including as we collaborate with classroom teachers. When thinking about students seeking and receiving information, we must not only secure their literal access; we must also prepare them with the knowledge, ability, and skills to locate, critically evaluate, and responsibly use information. Whether teaching information literacy skills and digital citizenship, providing reader's advisory or reading instruction, facilitating makerspaces or writing workshops, we should ask ourselves: *How are we educating students about their intellectual freedom rights? How are we protecting and feeding their intellectual curiosity? How are we empowering them to be intellectually liberated?*

> *"Intellectual freedom empowers young people to make smart decisions and solve real-world problems."*
>
> —Barbara M. Jones

VIGNETTE: SCHOOL LIBRARIANSHIP AS INTELLECTUAL LIBERATION

Julia Torres

A lot of kids in my community have serious trauma around the act of reading, because they've been told that if they can't read at a certain Lexile level or master fluency with certain texts, then they are not good enough. They are always being told that excellence is beyond their reach and that they are not as good as students in other places. *You are not at their level. You need to rise up to their level.* But, what does this mean when the measure is based on cultural capital that our students do not know about? What does it mean when students are evaluated based on reading stories or narratives from cultures that are completely foreign to them?

It is not fair or liberatory to educate students to continually perform to a standard of excellence that is external to their lived reality and may not even be relevant for the lives that they plan on living. Rather than talking vaguely about college and career readiness, we need to think specifically about how our educational systems, programming, and content are relevant to students' lives.

What I try to do in my work as a school librarian is support developing readers that have been traumatized. I do this by helping students encounter, read, and develop a relationship with language that centers their literacies, lived realities, and experiences, one that highlights the excellence found in people and cultures that look like them and share their heritage. By getting them to see that there is a rich culture of readers and writers that they can connect to culturally, linguistically, and ethnically, I am helping them become intellectually free.

This work is particularly important since it is far too common that classroom teachers strictly control what students *must* read in order to receive a grade that is academic currency, while so much of what they *want* to read is relegated to a book club or an activity for students to do on the side. I understand the appeal of teaching whole class novels. There's limited time, and it seems like the most expedient way to ensure that no one gets left behind since everyone is reading the same book at the same time. But, more often than not, it leaves most of the control in the hands of the teacher rather than finding ways for students to take control over their own learning. We think we're doing students a favor, because we're teaching them skills, but if you look at the bigger picture, we are limiting their ability to choose for themselves, to have a fully fleshed out, healthy, inclusive, and diverse relationship with reading and language.

Our increased circulation statistics have revealed that the collection and my progress with developing the collection and advocating for #OwnVoices has supported many more kids in having a longer standing relationship with words that will affect them for the rest of their lives. Furthermore, as I work to build back up students' confidence in their own skill set, I also educate educators about the skills and talents that our students are bringing to the school experience rather than students needing to conform or change something about who they are in order to meet the status quo and to meet standards that they have had no part in formulating.

Complementing student access to more expansive and representative reading, I simultaneously help develop and encourage student writing so that they may see themselves as creators of content rather than primarily consumers. When doing so, we have to be cognizant that there's still so much adultism built within the policies and practices in the school system. Teachers are generally the purveyors of feedback. Even peer-editing checklists are so controlled versus having a more authentic readers or writers workshop. In a truly liberatory educational environment, we will see more freedom, more intellectual freedom, more freedom over their bodies, more freedom over what students' finished product looks like, more freedom over how students demonstrate learning. Part of that has involved redefining what students understand to be good writing. From a very early age, we indoctrinate students to believe that good writing is whatever the teacher says is good writing rather than understanding good writing is within them. My goal is for students to see: *I am a writer. What I need to do is define for myself what excellence looks like.*

Related to external measures, testing and grading are practices that withhold a lot of intellectual freedom, preventing students from exploring their intellectual curiosity. Most kids have come to equate learning with performance. They think of coming to school as doing what they're told. It's not fun. They don't like it. It makes a lot of them very miserable. And so, then what happens? You get a whole generation of people or multiple generations with a reflexive reaction against intellectualism and learning.

A shift I noticed when moving from being a language arts teacher to working as a school librarian is the fact that grades are no longer tied to participation. I walk down the hall, and people want to talk about books they love. They want to high five me. They want to hear readalouds. They want to go on field trips. They want to meet individually with me. It's a different energy, because I am no longer in the position of serving someone else's agenda. Now, I'm more in the authentic service of the students and their personally relevant learning than I was able to be when I served as a classroom teacher.

Being a school librarian is powerful exactly because of its potential to support the intellectual freedom of students in a unique way outside of the restrictions of other systems in schools such as mandated curriculum, grading, and standardized testing. This is why it is also essential that we in the profession collectively shed light on the fact that classroom teaching and school librarianship are predominantly White female fields. If we want to see change, we need to start by having critical conversations with educators and students about career choices. Working together, faculty, including school librarians. must put renewed effort into encouraging our students who identify as people of color or people from marginalized backgrounds to see education and school librarianship as viable career options. Through collaboration, we can ensure students have the knowledge, skills, and motivation within themselves to do this important work in schools and communities.

Julia is the school librarian at the Montbello Campus Library (6–12), Denver Public Schools, Denver, Colorado. One of Library Journal's *2020 Movers & Shakers and a former language arts teacher, Julia cofounded #disrupttexts, serves as a "Book Ambassador" for the Educator Collaborative, and regularly presents on educating for intellectual and physical liberation.*

Laws, Codes, and Policies

Throughout this courage section, we have explored areas of school library programs to interrogate with a lens for intellectual freedom, and in closing, we want to raise the importance of becoming aware of and updating policies. Questions to consider include the following:

- **What federal laws apply?** To start, make sure that you are familiar with FERPA (Family Educational Rights and Privacy ACT), CIPA (Children's Internet Protection Act), and COPPA (Children's Online Privacy Protection Act).

- **What state educational codes exist?** If you are unsure, search for and become familiar with your state's educational codes (e.g., California Education Code 48907 affirms public school students' right to exercise freedom of speech and the press).

- **What is covered in district board policies?** Locate and carefully study existing policies such as those related to curriculum, materials challenges, and more.

- **What other school library policies exist?** A library use and behavior policy? A privacy and confidentiality policy? When creating or reviewing policies, be aware that the *Intellectual Freedom Manual* dedicates a whole section to policies.

There are also helpful online resources such as ALA's Selection & Reconsideration Policy Toolkit for Public, School, & Academic Libraries (http://www.ala.org/tools/challengesupport/selectionpolicytoolkit).

By becoming knowledgeable about laws, codes, and policies, you may ensure that your practices are in proper alignment, which prepares you to face any future challenges. It also allows you the opportunity to advocate for potential policy changes. In many cases, local level policies may have been adopted in the past and may be in need of updating. Once you are aware of what is in place, you may use this information to start conversations with colleagues, administrators, and other stakeholders to make informed revisions, as necessary. In this way, you not only position yourself to defend challenges, but you may proactively create systemic changes that support intellectual freedom.

Starting the Work for Intellectual Freedom Right Where We Are

AASL's *National School Library Standards for Learners, School Librarians, and School Libraries* are based on six common beliefs, including the belief that "intellectual freedom is every learner's right" (AASL 2018b, 13).

School librarians are responsible for fostering one of America's most cherished freedoms: the freedom of speech and freedom to hear what others have to say. Learners have the right to choose what they will read, view, or hear. Learners are expected to develop the ability to think clearly, critically, and creatively about their choices, rather than allowing others to control their access to ideas and information. The school librarian's responsibility is to develop these dispositions in learners, educators, and other members of the learning community. (AASL 2018b, 13)

As you consider your responsibilities related to intellectual freedom, we encourage you to identify and claim the source of your passion, find ways to demonstrate your commitment, and explore areas that require your courage. We have shared some of our personal journey in learning and thinking more broadly about intellectual freedom, and yet our own work is far from over. There are practices that we plan to discuss with district colleagues, there are policies that we need to review and update, and there are fundamental changes that we must continually strive to make the educational experiences of students more intellectually liberating. We urge you to similarly start wherever you are, to embrace your vulnerability in honestly assessing the work that needs to be done to secure greater freedom for your students, and then to start the work.

Reflection Questions

1. What practices are you already doing to support the intellectual freedom of students and staff members in your school community, including ones that you may not have previously identified as relating to intellectual freedom?
2. In what ways can you more intentionally and actively maintain and advocate for intellectual freedom in your school community, both within and beyond the library?
3. What policies do you need to review and develop or update for your school and district? What do you need to read and learn more about?

References

Adams, Helen R. 2013. *Protecting Intellectual Freedom and Privacy in Your School Library*. Santa Barbara, CA: ABC-CLIO.

American Association of School Librarians. 2018a. *Defending Intellectual Freedom: LGBTQ+ Materials in School Libraries*. Chicago: American Association of School Librarians.

American Association of School Librarians. 2018b. *National School Library Standards for Learners, School Librarians, and School Libraries*. Chicago: American Library Association.

American Library Association. 2004. "The Freedom to Read Statement." *American Library Association*. Available at http://www.ala.org/advocacy/intfreedom /freedomreadstatement. Accessed October 1, 2020.

American Library Association. 2019. "Library Bill of Rights." *American Library Association*. Available at http://www.ala.org/advocacy/intfreedom/librarybill. Accessed October 1, 2020.

American Library Association. 2020a. "Code of Ethics." *American Library Association*. Available at http://www.ala.org/tools/ethics. Accessed October 1, 2020.

American Library Association. 2020b. "Office for Intellectual Freedom." *American Library Association*. Available at http://www.ala.org/aboutala/offices/oif. Accessed October 1, 2020.

American Library Association. 2020c. "The State of America's Libraries 2020: A Report from the American Library Association." Steve Zalusky, ed. Available at http://www.ala.org/news/state-americas-libraries-report-2020. Accessed October 1, 2020.

American Library Association. 2020d. "Top 10 Most Challenged Book Lists." *American Library Association*. Available at http://www.ala.org/advocacy/bbooks/frequentlychallengedbooks/top10. Accessed October 1, 2020.

Brennan, William J., Jr, and Supreme Court of the United States. 1982. *U.S. Reports: Board of Education v. Pico*, 457 U.S. 853. Periodical. Available at https://www.loc.gov/item/usrep457853. Accessed October 1, 2020.

Diaz, Johnny. 2020, February 3. "Librarians Could Face Charges for 'Age-Inappropriate' Material under Proposal." *New York Times*. Available at https://www.nytimes.com/2020/02/03/us/missouri-libraries-sexual-books.html. Accessed October 1, 2020.

Fletcher-Spear, Kristin, and Kelly Tyler, eds. 2014. *Intellectual Freedom for Teens*. Chicago: American Library Association.

Fortas, Abe, and Supreme Court of the United States. 1969. *U.S. Reports: Tinker v. Des Moines School Dist.*, 393 U.S. 503. Periodical. Available at https://www.loc.gov/item/usrep393503. Accessed October 1, 2020.

Jones, Barbara M. 2015. "What Is Intellectual Freedom?" In *Intellectual Freedom Manual*, 9th ed., ed. T. Magi, 3–13. Chicago: American Library Association.

Krosoczka, Jarrett J. 2018, October 26. "What's Appropriate for Kids to Read? There's Value in Exposing Them to the Tough Stuff." *Washington Post*. Available at https://www.washingtonpost.com/entertainment/books/whats-appropriate-for-kids-to-read-theres-value-in-exposing-them-to-the-tough-stuff/2018/10/25/148f0b80-d7b9-11e8-83a2-d1c3da28d6b6_story.html. Accessed October 1, 2020.

Magi, Trina, ed. 2015. *Intellectual Freedom Manual*. 9th ed. Chicago: American Library Association.

Oltmann, Shannon. 2017. "Creating Space at the Table: Intellectual Freedom Can Bolster Diverse Voices." *Library Quarterly* 87(4): 410–418. doi: 10.1086/693494.

Right to Read Defense Committee v. School Committee of the City of Chelsea, 1978 D. Mass. Available at https://law.justia.com/cases/federal/district-courts/FSupp/454/703/2135164. Accessed October 1, 2020.

U.S. District Court for the District of Massachusetts. 1978. *Right to Read Defense Committee v. School Committee of the City of Chelsea*, 454 F. Supp. 703. Available at https://law.justia.com/cases/federal/district-courts/FSupp/454 /703/2135164. Accessed October 1, 2020.

Whelan, Debra. 2009. "A Dirty Little Secret: Self-Censorship." *School Library Journal*. Available at https://www.slj.com/?detailStory=a-dirty-little-secret -self-censorship. Accessed October 1, 2020.

PART II

Courage: Core Values in Action

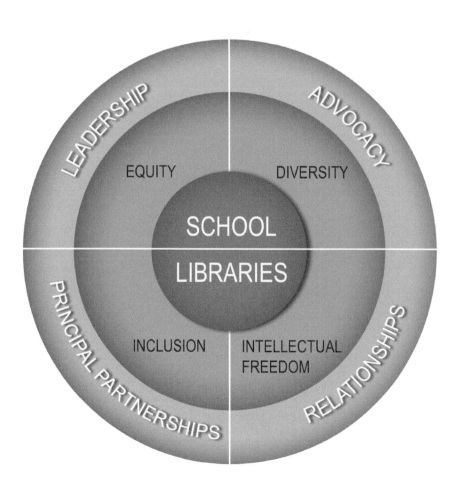

CHAPTER 5

Relationships

*Jennifer Sturge with Stacy Allen
and Sandy Walker*

Relationships are the taproot of a strong school community.

Sparking a Passion for Libraries

Life was good for me at the back of the bus until sixth grade. I, Sandy Walker, was surrounded by my best friends, our bus driver played whatever cassette tapes we provided, and the trip to school was always filled with laughter. At least until Vinny turned to everyone with a ball of tin foil and asked, "Who's in?"

Naively and excitedly, I thought his mom made brownies. I quickly realized my mistake as he unraveled the pills. I watched as everyone reached over, lifted a pill, and swallowed. Five pairs of eyes turned to me. I had a decision to make. And I had to make it quick. I guess I could have thought about my father's lectures about the exemplary conduct I need to display as a Black male in America, or the stories of hardship and sacrifice my parents endured to move us to a safer neighborhood. I also could have thought of the church songs my mother often sang about heaven and all it will take to get there. But in that moment and in that space, I thought about Spider-Man.

I was an avid reader. Our school librarian often pulled me aside during checkout and offered me the newest book. She always laughed that I was her job security, not that I knew what that meant. One day, she told me to check out the new rack and the new comic novel. As I spun the rack to see how many rotations I could get with one push, it stopped right at a hardcover book called *Spider-Man*. I had seen some pictures of him, but I never knew he had an actual book. He was surrounded by menacing figures, including a guy with sparks coming out of his hand, another guy with four metallic arms, and a guy with limbs made of sand. Something about such bleak odds of success for this little guy dressed in such a brightly colored suit intrigued me.

There would be no sleeping for me that night. That anthology of Spider-Man original stories hooked me. The Sinister Six, as the evil group came to be known, was and still is united by the thirst for Spider-Man's death. Spider-Man is not the strongest guy around. He is also a teenager named Peter Parker who struggles to fit in at school as he deals with guilt over his uncle's death and takes care of old Aunt May. Despite all of the obstacles in his life, including the desire to just lead a normal life, Peter Parker confronts every challenge because it's simply the right thing to do. As the Peter Parker principle states: "With great power comes great responsibility." My school librarian special ordered every Spider-Man collection she could find for me.

At the back of the bus, I was not surrounded by the Sinister Six, and no one was going to zap me with any kind of ray beam or threaten to come after my "Aunt May." I was after all surrounded by my friends. However, I knew I was facing the greatest challenge of my life, and I did not have any web shooters with me. Calmly and quietly, I got up and walked to the front of the bus to find a new seat.

Spider-Man taught me the value of conviction and purpose. I learned that deep relationships are forged through the sharing of our personal stories and ourselves: our strengths, our weaknesses, and our purpose for existence. I don't know what would have happened on the bus that day if I had not known Spider-Man's story. I do know that the relationship I had with him equipped me with the confidence to be brave, to be an individual, and to be a source of strength for others. Positive relationships benefit our own happiness. They are also an impetus for striving to change the world.

> *"If there's one thing my kids know, it's that I'm there for them. The relationships we've built through books is just a platform to show them that I'm listening, I'm invested in them, and I'm in their corner."*
>
> —Shelby Denhof

Relationships Connect Us All

In a school library and outside of the school library, relationships are everything. They can change the world for children and adults, including school librarians. The act of making a connection, feeling and being connected, is something that humans strive for whether it is a relationship with a place, pet, parent, colleague, or student.

We offer three very distinct voices in this chapter. Those voices belong to Stacy Allen, Jennifer Sturge, and Sandy Walker. We work together, have very different roles in our school system, and have built a relationship. By the end of this chapter, we sincerely hope that you will recognize how three people with three very different job responsibilities built a relationship based on shared values and enacting courage that positively impacts Calvert County Public Schools (CCPS) students, staff, librarians, and school community.

Collaboration and Strong Relationships among Colleagues

"Successful collaborative education is about relationships. Relationships are an essential part of the teaching process" (Coleman 2020, 17). We collaborated on this chapter because of the relationships that we have built

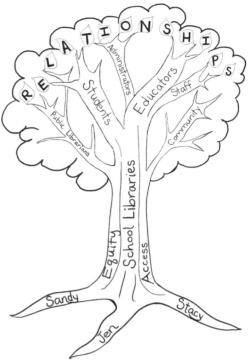

Figure 5.1 We collaborate because we truly feel that when relationships are strong between colleagues, it translates into student growth, student learning, and a positive school environment for everyone. (Graphic by Stacy Allen)

over the years. We're colleagues and friends; we've seen each other rant, rave, cry, bang our heads against the wall, and laugh hysterically. So, why are the three of us collaborating on a chapter about relationships in school libraries? We're a team. As a team we each bring our own area of expertise to the table. Jen brings the knowledge of school libraries and literacy. Sandy brings his expertise and voice on equity and diversity and building spaces for students who are marginalized. Stacy uses her powerful voice to advocate for those who, because of a disability, don't always see themselves represented in our school community. In our work, we have discovered powerful ways in which the relationships we have built together benefit our school community.

We collaborate with each other to make our libraries safe havens for our students and places where students can feel comfortable and confident. Our collaboration started in the fall of 2018 with Sandy and Jen presenting the Southern Poverty Law Center's Learning for Justice Social Justice Standards (2016) to the school librarians. Throughout this process, we worked together to not only ensure that our curriculum became a place for social justice, but that the librarians to whom we entrusted the teaching of the curriculum had a deep and meaningful understanding of what it means to promote, live, breathe, and teach social justice in our libraries. The collaboration between Sandy and Jen continues during the professional development with school librarians throughout the year. Social justice and diversity of collection development have become a theme that we continually address. Because of this collaboration, school librarians have started the process of conducting diversity audits in our libraries and a massive weeding of old, outdated, and unused books that do not represent the students we serve.

Sparks Become Flames

My passion for libraries as places of equity was solidified when I was just seven years old. Our public library held a bookmark contest. As a budding young artist, I, Jen, spent hours drawing six hearts in varying shades of yellow, orange, and red on a piece of paper and wrote "One for all, all for free . . . Libraries!" on my bookmark. To everyone's surprise (including my mother's) my bookmark won the contest. It was printed and put on the circulation desk for everyone to take as they checked out books. That was the moment when I connected to our public library.

It only takes an instant to spark a relationship, and that spark, for me, took place over a bookmark. After that, I spent as much time as I possibly could in the public library and in the school library, reading everything I could possibly check out. My world grew as my love of reading grew. I can even remember hiding beneath the sheets drying on the clothesline in the summer to devour *Tiger Eyes* and *Forever* by Judy Blume—something that was forbidden and only confessed to my mother almost thirty years later.

I've passed on my love of the library. My son is involved in the public library's Teen Advisory Council of Students (TACOS). He looks forward to the monthly meetings—mostly for the pizza—but also to plan events for teens in the library. He learned to play Dungeons and Dragons at the library and participates in Teen Book Club monthly. My hope is that wherever he ends up for college and beyond, he will find a home in his local library, too.

"Relationship flat-out trumps competence in building trust" (Rath 2008, 85). As a school librarian, I built relationships with students, some of whom I still keep in touch with all these years later! That spark that started my relationship with libraries still lights my life as strongly today as it did when I was seven years old.

This chapter is all about relationships and how they spark imagination and how curiosity can ignite into a flame. Along with these sparks, this chapter is also about using the potential of our school libraries for powerful collaboration and commitment to building lasting change so sparks of curiosity become the flames of lifelong learning and literacy for all.

Commitment to Building Relationships

You can't write about school librarianship without writing about how building relationships with students often centers around books. After all, the school librarian has the power to suggest, discuss, and recommend something that is often very needed in students' lives—literature and information. Lisa Cron writes in *Wired for Story: The Writer's Guide to Using Brain Science to Hook Readers from the Very First Sentence*: "Story is the language of experience, whether it's ours, someone else's, or that of fictional characters. Other people's stories are as important as the stories we tell ourselves. Because if all we ever had to go on was our own experience, we'd never make it out of onesies" (2012, 13).

> *"Students are our priority. No matter what else we do, what programs we create, what books we choose, everything we do in some way should further their development as lifelong learners, users, and producers of knowledge. We build relationships with teachers because they are the gateway to the students, but we also must build direct connections to students."*
>
> —Hilda K. Weisburg

Building a diverse collection goes a long way to making libraries welcoming to students. So, too, does making our collections and library materials accessible to all readers, including those with disabilities. In my position as an assistive technology specialist for our district, I, Stacy, collaborate with Jen to ensure that all students can access library resources and build their own relationships with books. Meeting students where they are (Wathen 2018) can take the form of anticipating student needs by having an accessible collection that appeals to reader preference and ability. Taking a Universal Design for Learning approach to building a library that works well for people with disabilities will result in a collection and environment that better supports everyone. We can build relationships when students see themselves or those they love reflected back on the pages of books.

This is the approach we have taken in CCPS to ensure that everyone sees themselves reflected in our collections. We can enter worlds where characters look and act like us, or we can enter worlds that are nothing like what we know for ourselves. Both are needed and necessary. This is why we consider equity, diversity, and accessibility in our collection development. In the process, we strengthen relationships between readers and books, students and librarians, and resources and learning.

When accessibility is considered in the design and creation of all our materials and spaces, we welcome students, whoever they are, and reinforce that diversity is normal.

Some possibilities to consider in making accessible libraries:

- Multiple means of access to stories
  - Audiobooks/listening centers
  - Large print books
  - Web tools for read-alouds
  - Graphic novels
  - Closed captions for every video (this supports neurodiversity in general and is essential for people who are deaf or hard of hearing)
- Considerations for communication
  - Picture symbols at checkout and other locations
  - Core language boards or posters to support students who use nonverbal communication
- Space
  - Variable options for seating and standing
  - Space for students using mobility devices (e.g., walkers, wheelchairs, crutches, and canes) to safely navigate and access materials

Students with and without disabilities may be interested in books that are above their ability to decode the text, and accessibility tools can make reading those books possible. And when reading becomes possible, the sparks become flames, and a love of reading is born. Creating libraries that are safe and open spaces for all is a vital part of building relationships with every student in our buildings.

Building Relationships Based on a Commitment to Robust Curriculum

As we moved through our professional development work focused on diversity and equity, CCPS school librarians began to think deeply about building relationships. These relationships in the school district take on many different forms. One is building strong communities within our school libraries. In order to make this happen, a small team of amazing school librarians came together to rewrite our elementary curriculum.

Elementary Library Curriculum

In our elementary schools, we start relationship building with and among students from the very beginning of the year in every grade. In kindergarten, we begin our library year with reading *All Are Welcome* by Alexandra Penfold and start the conversation about diversity, respecting each other, and celebrating our identities. We continue that conversation in our first units in the school library throughout every grade. Our essential question reads: "How can we recognize and celebrate the differences in each other?" We focus on the AASL Shared Foundations of Include and Explore (AASL 2018) and the Learning for Justice Social Justice Anchor Standards of Identity and Diversity.

From the beginning, we invite our kindergarten students into our libraries, making it a welcome space for starting relationships. We discuss our favorite pages, our special talents, and what we can teach each other. We see this as our first opportunity to start building positive relationships between our students and ourselves. In first, second, and third grade we continue to build on these relationship themes by introducing community with read-alouds such as *What I Like about Me* by Allia Zobel-Nolan and Miki Sakamoto and *The Juice Box Bully* by Maria Dismondy. In fourth and fifth grades, we really dig into developing empathy by utilizing Nearpod and Nearpod resources and having students ask the question, "How can I make the world a better place?" All of this happens in the first few weeks of school.

By starting off the year thinking about our identity, our diversity, and our community, we foster positive relationships with and among our students that continue throughout their elementary years. Our curriculum is a direct result of the implementation of the Learning for Justice Social Justice Standards and the work that our school librarians have done to promote social justice, identity, and diversity in our schools. This is a constant work in progress. Watching the relationships form because of understanding and empathy proves to us how important it is to take courageous steps to enact change and to continue to move forward with change even in the face of adversity in the world outside of school.

Relationship Building with Content-Area Educators

"Successful collaboration is characterized as an equal partnership between the classroom teacher and the teacher-librarian. This collaboration requires that both the classroom teacher and the teacher-librarian are committed to working together and that they have a common mission."

—Darcy McNee and Elaine Radmer

As school librarians focus on the knowledge and skills that are required to become a productive member of society, the collaboration that takes place between librarians and classroom educators is one of the most powerful relationships in our schools. Effective collaboration that takes place on a regular basis and in a meaningful manner can result in students being future ready. As Judi Moreillon (2018) notes, students who have regular access to learning through classroom-library collaboration for instruction are:

- Culturally literate.
- Digital and media literate.

- Information literate.
- Creative.
- Innovative.
- Critical thinkers.
- Problem solvers.
- Proficient readers.

Students benefit from school librarians' and classroom teachers' collaborative instruction for project-based and other deep learning experiences by building dispositions such as adaptability, confidence, curiosity, flexibility, gratitude, grit, imagination, and more (Moreillon 2018, 2).

Building relationships through collaboration with content-area educators involves working together, solving problems, completing tasks, and creating projects (AASL 2018, 29). Through relationships, we foster new learning opportunities for our students and can achieve amazing results. Hilda Weisburg (2017) writes, "Many librarians have struggled with getting teachers to work with them but you will never be regarded as a leader if you work alone in your library" (47).

The Courage to Take Risks

The courage in collaboration with classroom educators comes from the knowledge that as school librarians we may very well have to step out of our comfort zone to meet the needs of classroom educators. We may need to approach teachers who have never utilized the school library in the past. We may need to think outside of the box for scheduling to allow collaboration to happen. School librarians may need to have the courage to advocate for a more flexible schedule with their administration in order to make classroom-library collaboration a priority. Each of those acts takes courage. Every opportunity to collaborate won't be perfect. Some collaboration may look more like coordination, but those efforts are positive steps in the right direction.

"Don't eat at your desk. Eat lunch with teachers. Sneak in some conversation
about information literacy and programming that is available in the library.
Really talk up those resources over a mouth full of salad."

—Donna Mignardi and Jen Sturge

School librarians need to build strong relationships with classroom teachers. This can mean offering to collaborate in the library or in the classroom depending on the teachers' comfort level. In our district, our high school and middle school librarians attend our subject area team meetings and are a part of the planning process whenever possible.

Donna Mignardi, a school librarian at Calvert High School, is a regular attendee at the English department meetings. Through her regular attendance, she learned that the department was going to be moving toward a model of student choice in book selection. Immediately, she started thinking about how she could impact this decision and how she could collaborate with the classroom educators. Her thinking sparked a school-wide movement that promoted reading choice and became a collaboration across every grade level in the school. She and her English teacher collaborators started a book speed dating system in the school library.

Donna very purposefully engaged with her teachers by approaching the English department chair about attending team meetings and sharing ideas she learned or thought would be great collaborative projects. She quickly realized that teachers sometimes overlooked collaboration with the librarian if their curriculum covered some aspect of information literacy. She carefully cultivated her relationships with not only the English department, but other departments across the school, and attends and participates in their planning meetings as often as possible. Her persistence paid off in building collaborative relationships that resulted in a school-wide culture of reading. Donna says, "I listen and offer help and resources when appropriate. I am as excited as the classroom educator when a lesson is successful and ask if I may visit the classroom to see the lesson in action. I became part of the team." These relationships are the foundation for exciting and successful collaborative activities throughout the school year.

"When school librarians coteach with classroom teachers and specialists, they support their principals' initiatives for change and improvement, and they support their colleagues' and their own professional learning" (Moreillon 2018, 33). Classroom-library collaboration for instruction supports school improvement, which in turn supports and builds positive relationships with administrators. Building relationships with administrators is incredibly important; these partnerships can make all the difference in the world.

VIGNETTE: EXPAND YOUR INFLUENCE OUTSIDE OF LIBRARY WALLS

Tamara Cox

Sixteen years ago, I started my career in education as a seventh-grade history teacher. I quickly realized that my students were more engaged, effective learners when information was presented as a story, so we read several novels each year in my classroom. Using novels in my teaching and seeing the power of story is what made me consider becoming a school librarian. Once I had a few years of teaching under my belt, I began to have the itch to expand my influence beyond the four walls of my classroom. My research into a career change revealed that school librarian is a critical needs area in my state of South Carolina, which brought financial help in earning a master's in library and information science degree.

My transition from the classroom to the library was made smoother because I already had a good working relationship with my administrators and other faculty members. That year I made sweeping changes, including a significant weeding of materials, a switch to genre organization in both fiction and nonfiction, new furniture, and an emphasis on collaboration. None of these successful changes would have been possible without administrator support.

After four years as a librarian, I spent three years as an instructional technologist, part of a district-wide 1:1 device deployment. Although I treasure those years and the personal growth that came from that time, I could not pull my heart away from my life's purpose: sharing the love of reading and serving students in the library. When one of my district's librarians decided to retire, I knew this was my chance to go back to what I love.

Shortly after I was hired as the librarian at Wren High School, there was an administration change. From my experience in my first school librarian position, I knew that a strong relationship between the librarian and administrator was vital for success. As soon as I heard the news, I reached out to the new principal, Dr. Seth Young, to request a meeting. I had big plans for that first year, and I knew I would need his support to make it happen. We met and shared our goals for the library program. I was relieved and excited that he saw the library as an integral part of instruction. He was also on board with the big changes that I wanted to make in the library program.

Numerous studies spanning multiple states and decades have shown that a high-quality library program positively impacts student achievement, graduation rates, and mastery of academic standards, but does your administrator know this? It is part of our mission to share that with all of our school's stakeholders. For many librarians, it may feel uncomfortable to be the one to start this conversation, but it is imperative. I share articles and research about the role and impact of school libraries as well as collecting and sharing data specific to my school. We must put aside our humility and share our successes, whether it is an effective lesson, published article, or educational award. Each time we share our success, we have the potential to change someone's opinion of what a school librarian can contribute to a school and break the stereotypes about our role.

I am fortunate that my administration does see me as a leader, and I work hard to maintain their trust in me. I have been honored to represent our school as a presenter and speaker at several conferences, and my administration has encouraged those efforts. Dr. Young and I have even presented together about the administration and library program partnership. Although I consider myself lucky to work with my current administration, I also know there are concrete, practical steps librarians (and administrators) can take to build or improve on this partnership if this is not the current circumstance at your school.

Supporting the school library program comes from administrator acts both big and small. Dr. Young is a very supportive administrator, and there are many ways that he shows his support. He and other administrators frequently stop by the library to ask if I need anything. They come in to observe lessons and programs, participate in reading programs, include me on school-wide committees, and communicate the expectation to faculty that they want teachers to collaborate with me. They protect my time and the resources in the school library so that I can focus on serving students and teachers instead of being drafted for peripheral tasks.

Administrator support has helped me to build relationships with teachers from many different subject levels and implement successful reading programs for our students and faculty. In order to safeguard the positive relationship I have with administration, I provide regular reports on library lessons and events. I invite administration to observe and participate in the library programs. We meet regularly to ensure that my work in the library is helping the school meet our collective goals.

Ultimately, the benefits of a robust and effective school library program under the leadership of a certified librarian are undeniable and supported by research. Having administrative support and a commitment from all stakeholders is key. When administrators rethink the role of the school librarian and nurture collaboration with the librarian, your school can leverage the power of their librarian and see positive changes in student learning and achievement.

Tamara is the National Board–certified librarian at Wren High School in Piedmont, South Carolina. She is a 2020 Library Journal Mover and Shaker, 2019 SC School Librarian of the Year, finalist for SC Teacher of the Year, I Love My Librarian winner, and active member of the SC Association of School Librarians. Connect at @coxTL.

Get Involved for Professional Success

As school librarians, we are all too often an island, a solo act, alone in our buildings. By growing your personal learning network (PLN) locally and getting involved in your state, local, or national associations, you can build some amazing professional relationships. There are numerous opportunities to build professional networks at the state and national level. Even if you don't have a lot of time to commit to being a part of something larger, there are always small things you can do to grow connections in the larger library world. Here are just a few of them:

1. Attend a Twitter chat. You will be amazed at the ideas you can garner from one of the many school librarian Twitter chats that happen on a regular basis. Even if you are not ready to participate, watching the conversation unfold can be powerful.

2. Become members of school librarian Facebook groups.

3. Join your local and state library organizations. This is a great way to support each other and to connect with librarians in your community and across your state.

4. Attend state and national conferences. Not only will you learn a great deal, but you will have a chance to connect with people who share the same passion for school librarianship as you. There's something really powerful about a collective group coming together in the same place and space to learn and share.

5. Join the American Library Association (ALA) and the American Association of School Librarians (AASL). There are so many opportunities to build relationships by joining our national associations. Committees form throughout the year. You can get involved on the Connect platform and more.

6. Share! The more we share our work, the bigger our network will become. Sharing comes in all shapes and sizes. It can be as simple as sharing a lesson plan with a fellow librarian or signing up for a yearlong stint as a blogger for *Knowledge Quest*.

VIGNETTE: LIBRARIANSHIP: IT'S A CAREER AND A FRIENDSHIP

April Wathen and Brittany Tignor

How often is it that one can honestly say they enjoy work so much that the lines between work and life get blurred? In what career fields can one say that the fabric between colleagues and friendships is so tightly woven that one cannot even imagine life without the joy that some of your fellow colleagues, now close friends, bring to it? Welcome to the world of librarianship!

As a school librarian, it is not unusual to naturally feel as though you are working in a silo. Generally, school librarians are a "party of one" within their schools. In smaller districts, it is not unusual for their supervisors to lack a library background. Developing collaborative partnerships, participating in school library professional development, and seeking library leadership positions are largely left up to the school librarians looking to bring the best of their field to all stakeholders. Despite, or maybe because of, the individual nature of the job, librarians are naturally drawn to one another.

Many school librarians flock to conferences, flood virtual professional development groups, get involved in their state organizations, and become deeply rooted in their PLN as a way of making connections. Relationships in the world of a librarian are very important and lead to an increased knowledge base and an ability to provide topnotch experiences for their stakeholders. School librarians often value relationships with community members, faculty and staff, families, students, and each other. It is not unusual to strike up a conversation at a conference and develop a fast friendship that can last many years.

Enter our story of two librarians who became lifelong friends through librarianship, leadership, and a state association.

Our initial meeting was forgettable. Literally, we cannot remember the first time we actually met. April was a conference co-chairperson and was glad meetings became virtual as this allowed her to get involved in leadership. She lives in the southwestern part of the state and was unable to attend face-to-face meetings. She had a life outside of work and was a wife, mom, soccer coach, and scout leader, and did not have the time to travel to the face-to-face meetings. Brittany also began going to MASL meetings when they were offered virtually and later became a Member-at-Large. Brittany lives on the eastern side of the state, and as a school librarian in a small county, she wanted to meet other school librarians who were interested in learning from each other.

We have both held leadership positions in our state organizations. One of the first times we worked closely together was for the inaugural Maryland School Librarian of the Year Award developed by Brittany and her team. There was a marked time in our work that could have positively or negatively impacted our journey as effective leaders and friends. A candid, difficult conversation was needed in order to move on in a productive and effective way. This conversation was hard, and we were able to become stronger professionally and as friends who could better understand one another.

Since that first collaboration, we have worked together on many tasks for MASL and at one point served as president and past president at the same time. We have attended state and national conferences together and used the time in fun new cities as a chance to get to know one another and each other's families. We plan for our professional endeavors, support one another, and just share life together.

One of our fun planning memories was on the coach bus in Phoenix on our way to the ranch to see then AASL president Stephen Yates perform in a rodeo. During this ride, we plotted the agenda for our future leadership in office. This was also the same trip where a group of librarians, who have since become friends, shared a rental house for the duration of the conference and made many memories both on the professional and personal level.

We bring different strengths to our shared career field and state association. Brittany is really skilled at having a large organizational vision and is keen on sweeping improvements. April is happy to build relationships and get projects off of the ground to pass them on to the leadership who is ready to support them long term. What we share is that we are both open to new ideas and change and are always happy to provide support and encouragement to those looking to come aboard in a leadership capacity.

We both believe that together we are better. The keys to our professional and personal successes are sharing candidly and respectfully, and choosing to have difficult conversations. We host impromptu phone conversations and texts that may not make sense to the larger group. Those key behaviors create lasting relationships.

April is a national board-certified school librarian working at an elementary school in southern Maryland. April was named the Maryland School Librarian of the Year as well as a School Library Journal *Hero of Equitable Access. She has a passion for elevating student voice, purposeful instructional technology integration, building meaningful relationships, and being outdoors. Connect @ AprilWathen.*

Brittany is a high school librarian at Snow Hill, Maryland. She earned her bachelor's in English with a concentration in secondary education from Salisbury University and her master's in library and information studies from the University of Alabama. She is treasurer of the Maryland Association of School Librarians (MASL). Connect @BusyBLibrary.

Passion and Purpose, Commitment, Courage, and Collaborative Relationships—Oh, My!

As school librarians, we must continue to grow professionally, every day, every week, every month, and every year. We must build the relationships with our colleagues and our peers that help us maintain our passion and our purpose. We must be flexible and patient and "promote working productively with others to solve problems" (AASL 2018, 88). As Mary Catherine Coleman writes in her book *Collaborate*, we must "make (our) mark on people's hearts" (2020, 62). That is the power of a relationship—making a mark on people's hearts, taking that spark of curiosity and turning it into a flame of learning.

With the great power of being a school librarian comes great responsibility. It is within our power to do more, learn more, and be more so that all of our students and colleagues are successful. Courage and commitment arrive when school librarians step out of their comfort zones to collaborate with colleagues and classroom educators to meet the needs of the school community. It all starts with building and sustaining relationships. From the strong roots of our relationships, we grow stronger, become more visible, and serve our school community.

Reflection Questions

1. In the introductory paragraph, Sandy Walker wrote about Spider-Man's phrase "with great power comes great responsibility." In your role as a school librarian, what are some of the greatest responsibilities you have in terms of relationships with library stakeholders?

2. Stepping out of the library to build collaborative relationships with other educators takes courage. What steps will you take to build successful classroom-library partnerships and relationships that last with other library professionals?

3. In developing resource collections and lessons, how are you building the necessary partnerships to ensure that young people are connecting with diverse, relevant literature and information that is accessible for all?

References

American Association of School Librarians. 2018. *National School Library Standards for Learners, School Librarians, and School Libraries*. Chicago: American Library Association.

Coleman, Mary Catherine. 2020. *Collaborate*. Chicago: American Library Association.

Cron, Lisa. 2012. *Wired for Story: The Writer's Guide to Using Brain Science to Hook Readers from the Very First Sentence.* Berkeley, CA: Ten Speed.

Learning for Justice. 2016. "Social Justice Standards: The Teaching Tolerance Anti-Bias Framework." *Southern Poverty Law Center.* Available at https://www.learningforjustice.org/sites/default/files/2020-09/TT-Social-Justice-Standards-Anti-bias-framework-2020.pdf. Accessed February 16, 2021.

Moreillon, Judi. 2018. *Maximizing School Librarian Leadership: Building Connections for Learning and Advocacy.* Chicago: American Library Association.

Rath, Tom. 2008. *Strengths-Based Leadership: Great Leaders, Teams, and Why People Follow.* New York: Gallup.

Wathen, April. 2018. "The New Librarian: How I Use Tech to Build Relationships." *eSchool News.* Available at https://www.eschoolnews.com/2018/05/15/the-new-librarian-how-i-use-tech-to-build-relationships. Accessed October 1, 2020.

Weisburg, Hilda K. 2017. *Leading for School Librarians: There Is No Other Option.* Chicago: Neal-Schuman.

CHAPTER 6

Principal–School Librarian Partnerships

Kelly Gustafson and M. E. Shenefiel

Principals are our most important allies.

Our Common Ground

A strong alliance built between the school librarian and the principal is key to the academic success of an educational program. Strong library programs can positively impact student learning when principals and school librarians work together (Scholastic 2016, 6). This collaborative partnership seems natural given how much principals and librarians have in common. Both are focused on the big picture. Both see what's happening at the building level and use that insight to make connections across the curriculum.

In addition, both principals and school librarians have working relationships with all employees in the building as opposed to just working with one grade level or department. Principals care for their staff and encourage and promote professional development. Librarians recognize that classroom teachers, specialists, and support staff have information and resource needs that include, and extend beyond, the curriculum. Learners are not just students; adults serving in schools are learners, too. Both principals and librarians value a culture of collaboration. As a curriculum expert, the role of the school librarian is truly to bring together resources and opportunities for meaningful learning experiences across the curriculum.

Most importantly, both principals and school librarians advocate for the student. Both are in a position to forge relationships with every student. The dynamics of these relationships differ from the relationships that classroom teachers may have with students. Classroom teachers care for students on both personal and academic levels but are also directly accountable for the achievement of curricular goals and student growth through instruction and standardized assessment. Without this added pressure, the school librarian and the principal can often forge relationships with students that are more relaxed. Principals and librarians are able to focus more on the personal interests or concerns of the students both inside and outside of the classroom.

Connecting with Purpose

> *"More than ever, librarians serve to make connections."*
>
> —Brian R. Miller

School librarians see possibilities and create connections. "The role of the library and librarians has evolved in the information age. More than ever, librarians serve to make connections: We make connections between teachers and connections between content areas. These connections put isolated skills into real-life practice. Principals serve in a similar role as instructional leaders. When the principal and librarian are tightly aligned in the vision for learning in a school, they can serve as a team that helps promote integration and connections between teachers, students, content, and skills" (Miller 2020). School librarians connect learners to resources. We connect curricula to authentic learning experiences. We connect the community inside of the classroom to the community outside of the classroom. The most powerful connection a school librarian can make is with their principal. When this connection is strong, the principal will be open to possibilities that can benefit all stakeholders: students, staff, families, and community.

The traditional role of the school librarian is really no longer applicable, yet many educational stakeholders, including school principals, still have this narrow perception. Traditionally, the school librarian may have been solely responsible for managing and circulating collections. They may have had a cooperative relationship with school staff, providing resources and support when asked, but for many that was the extent of the services that school librarians provided. As noted in school librarian research, "throughout the standards issued over the past fifty years, a common and developing strand is that of the active instructional role of the library media specialist" (Church 2008, 3). Many principals don't recognize or understand the school librarian's instructional partner role and leadership potential. As a result, the librarian is still perceived as this antiquated stereotype.

Often there is also a disconnect between the perceived role of the school librarian in the educational community and the school librarian's skill set. In school library training programs, librarians are taught that we are essential to the educational community. We learn how to create learning plans that cross the curriculum. We are trained to foster collaborative relationships and advocate for students. We understand the importance of traditional, digital, and information literacies, and we come prepared to provide collaborative instruction in these skills. We learn to advocate for equity of access and diverse perspectives. School librarians who are fresh out of master's degree programs sometimes experience a rude awakening when they are hired for their first school library job and realize that the school's expectations of the school librarian don't rise to the bar that they have set for themselves.

The most effective way to bridge this gap is to develop a strong and trusting relationship with the school principal. In fact, this relationship is essential if school librarians want to have the most impact on students and colleagues. Principals set the direction for everything that happens in the building. They control resources, guide the school climate, and set the schedule. In short, school principals are responsible for the conditions for successful educational programs, including the library program.

School librarians are professionals, committed to the important work that we do. This commitment to the profession means that we are proactive and intentional about professional development. We stay informed of current trends, tools, and resources. We are aware of district initiatives and building goals, and familiar with the curricular and strategic goals of all of the departments in their school, not just the library. When principals recognize our skill set, school librarians can spread their influence throughout the learning community.

Seeing Every Student

The mission of our school district is "focused on learning for every student, every day" (Pine-Richland School District 2020). This simple syntax has complex implications. All employee decisions, regardless of role, come down to one question: "How will this decision impact teaching and learning for each individual learner?" As librarians in our district, each lesson we teach and each resource we choose must positively impact individual students.

At the time of this writing, the 2020–2021 school year is beginning, and school communities across the United States, and beyond, are grappling with finding the best way to provide our students with an education that will allow them to be successful in life. The first half of 2020 turned a magnifying glass on issues of equity, diversity, and inclusion among our students. Although school librarians have traditionally championed these core values, the double punch of COVID-19 closures and the increased awareness of racial inequities in the United States have catapulted these issues to the forefront of our collective educational agenda.

This year, on top of the "normal" back-to-school struggles, such as scheduling and staffing, school principals faced challenges of blended and virtual learning models, serious health and safety concerns, and racial tension. School principals and librarians can be allies in this struggle. School principals want effective teams that collaborate to provide the best educational opportunities for their students. School librarians want to be an integral part of that team so we can have the greatest impact on teaching and learning. An alliance between the librarian and principal benefits both, but ultimately students are the primary benefactors.

Drastic changes have been made to the educational model in an effort to mitigate the effects of COVID-19. Many schools have adopted a model that involves some type of online learning. School librarians have found that their spaces have been repurposed and staffing has been reduced. In the face of these challenges, school librarians remain steadfast in their commitment to provide equitable access to resources for all students. Lack of resources, insufficient infrastructure, or ineffective communication can prevent students from participating in learning activities and social interactions. School librarians are experts in finding resources that meet the curricular needs of the classroom teacher and student. So, while a classroom teacher might not be able to use a favorite resource or tool, the librarian should be able to find a suitable alternative that is accessible to all students.

Courage

"To be influential, (a leader) needs to be self-aware, focused, and competent, in order to be able to develop strong relationships and partnerships, in order to exhibit trust, honesty, and respect. One is not merely born with these attributes, but rather they can be developed and learned over time."

—Ken Haycock

Learning to Lead

Principals who value school librarians have a high expectation for those librarians to be leaders within their school or district. Whether you are completely new to the school library profession or a seasoned veteran in the field, one of the most important leadership practices you can establish is a habit of self-reflection. The school library profession is ever-changing just as information and technologies are ever-changing. What had seemed like an educational innovation just a few years ago could now be an outdated tool. What was once a commonly held belief can now seem hurtful or even dangerous. We have to be better, but in order to be better we have to be intentional about being aware. We increase our professional awareness by attending conferences, reading journals, and engaging with other professionals on social media. This idea is exemplified through our current endeavor to promote diverse literature and foster a culture of inclusivity. Many of us are just now opening our eyes to the once seemingly unnoticed racist messages in the favorite stories of our childhoods. School librarians need to be the leaders who speak up and question long-standing beliefs about these texts and provide alternatives that allow all students to feel included.

If we truly want to best serve our students and community, we have to continuously reflect on our efforts, resources, and learning activities to make sure they serve the best interests of all of our patrons. This practice can sometimes feel uncomfortable—especially when we admit to ourselves that we have room to improve. True leaders are never satisfied with the status quo. To librarian colleagues who are teaching the same lessons they taught ten years ago and still feel safe in a stereotypical "shushing librarian" role, Carolyn Foote says you have to "examine our own 'sacred cow'" (2015, 27). We cannot be the leaders our principals need us to be if we do not have the courage to take risks that will benefit our students.

Courageous Partnerships

Many principals may not perceive their school librarians as an essential collaborative partner and building leader. In fact, principals who do understand the unique role of school librarians are more likely to have learned that from experience rather than through any principal preparation programs (Hartzell 2007). This means that, in many cases, school librarians have to be proactive and initiate the communication process with their principals. Initially, there may be a period of time in which the librarian will have to design innovative instructional programming and educate the principal about their value within the school community. Building this alliance with your principal can take courage.

In order for transformative change to happen, librarians need to be intentional about cultivating this relationship. Getting to know your principal and developing an understanding of their leadership style is essential. Yet for many, reaching out to their principal can be intimidating. As educators who see the big picture, librarians walk the fine line of wanting to assert ourselves in terms of how we can help, but not wanting to inconvenience our principals who are juggling a myriad of problems on any given day.

Principals focus on management strategies to be more effective instructional leaders. This requires a strategic approach to the daily tasks scheduled within the calendar. Supervising and delegating action steps to accomplish project goals requires a laser focus. In fact, the role of the school leader is to expect interruptions from phone calls and unplanned visits to the office. The reality of the phrase "Do you have a minute?" can mean two things for a principal. Often the question is not literal and the minute extends beyond 60 seconds with the presentation of the problem or idea. Also, the request usually leads to another task being added to the list of considerations for new ideas or projects. Although the question has a negative connotation, the effective leader seeks out the details following the request because an open-door policy promotes limitless boundaries for educators who are solving problems and seeking continuous improvement. Principals who share their management style and work performance preferences with building-level educators create a communication model based on the strengths of their undivided attention.

School principals may not always be current with the latest trends in curriculum resources, technology tools, or issues of intellectual freedom, whereas school librarians are immersed in these topics. The opportunity to teach the supervisor is an effective way to manage in reverse. Librarians can train principals to look for diverse literature within classroom collections or address copyright issues within staff work procedures. This may seem precarious, but it is part of being willing to teach the principal the tools to achieve results in managing the school as an instructional leader.

Vignette: Be a Game Changer

Beth Shenefiel

"Principals are typically not aware of the instructional potential of the library media specialist."

—*Audrey Church*

Sometimes, however, you just luck out.

In the spring of 2018, our school board announced that we would be hiring two new principals, one of whom was a school library advocate working toward a doctoral degree with an emphasis on school libraries. I greedily hoped she would be assigned to my building, but instead she was assigned to one of the primary schools. She would, however, serve as the administrative liaison for our library department, and as the department chairperson, I would be working closely with her to lead the department.

Coincidentally, a month or two later I was asked by the Pennsylvania School Library Association (PSLA) to serve on a committee to revise the Guidelines for Pennsylvania School Libraries. As I read through the list of committee members, I saw a familiar name. At some point, it dawned on me that the name was familiar because she was the new principal who had just been hired by our district (and not so coincidentally, the coauthor of the chapter you are now reading). Kelly and I met face to face for the first time while completing this important work. Her reputation in the school library world had preceded her and, to my surprise, mine had preceded me as well. She was an administrator who was active in our state school library association and had testified in support of school libraries at the state and national levels. She had also published articles about the partnerships between principals and school librarians. Kelly was so positive and enthusiastic about school libraries that I knew having her lead with me would give our department a push out of our comfort zones and onto a path of continuous improvement.

In the spring of 2019, I invited Kelly to be my guest at the PSLA annual conference in Hershey, Pennsylvania. (Side note: If you attend professional conferences at the state or national level, consider inviting your administrators. It's a wonderful opportunity for them to learn about the complex and vital role of the school librarian.) At about this same time, AASL announced it would be creating a special committee for school administrators. "The 'AASL School Leader Collaborative: Administrators & School Librarians Transforming Teaching and Learning' is a two-year initiative that aims to strengthen AASL's collaboration with school administrators" (Habley 2019). Knowing her commitment to school libraries, I nominated Kelly for this committee. When (naturally) she was accepted to the committee, it was now her turn to return the favor, and I was able to attend the 2019 AASL National Conference in Louisville, Kentucky, as her guest.

We began the 2019–2020 school year with a flurry of activity as we welcomed two new librarians to the district and partnered to lead the department in completing a district-led in-depth review of our library program. We are the smallest department in the district, so those two librarians made up a third of our department. It's amazing how quickly a relationship can build when two people are leading a small group to complete a large-scale project with implications for years to come.

We were still getting to know one another, but every interaction that Kelly and I had reaffirmed our common belief that school libraries are essential for schools to be successful. Although we had different leadership styles, we very quickly became a powerful alliance poised to enact transformational change in the role of our librarians and the perception of our school library program. Having an administrative ally who embraced the unique and critical role of the school librarian renewed my commitment to building a stronger library program for our district.

It wasn't until we attended a professional development workshop in Grove City, Pennsylvania, that we began to understand how completely different we were. The workshop, sponsored by PSLA and delivered by David Bendekovic (2020), was entitled "Leading at Any Level: Leadership Development for Pennsylvania School Librarians." The workshop focused on leadership development through self-awareness. We sat next to each other as we worked through several personality inventories based on the book *Business Chemistry: Practical Magic for Crafting Powerful Work Relationships* by Kim Christfort and Suzanne Vickberg (2018). Two separate inventories assessed our styles when working with other people and our leadership orientation. Naturally, as one does while participating in this type of deep self-reflection while sitting next to a colleague, we began to compare our results. We laughed as we realized how polar opposite we were, especially when it came to leadership traits. The inventories explained a lot about why we interacted with each other the way we did. Yet we also realized that the combination seemed to work. Where one of us lacked the other had strength. Together, if we embraced these differences, we could be very effective leaders.

Kelly is truly a principal who understands the unique role that the school librarian plays within the learning community. Not only is she supportive of school libraries, but she's also passionate about them! If there is an educational problem that needs to be solved, the first idea that pops into her head is "How can the school librarians help with this?" When meeting with other educational stakeholders, she is always alert for opportunities to take advantage of the school library and librarian. The librarians in our district recognize that we are fortunate to work with an administrator who is passionate about the school library program.

Unfortunately for school librarians across the country, Kelly's view of the school library is the exception rather than the rule. Fortunately, it doesn't need to be that way. As stated by Gary Hartzell, Kelly's view of the library program is based on positive experiences with one school librarian from her past, a school librarian who made the effort to teach Kelly the value of school libraries and of building a culture of reading within her school. All school librarians have the potential to be this game changer. It takes courage, commitment, and real effort to strategically build a relationship with principals so that they can recognize the unique contributions of the school librarian.

Beth (she/her) is the librarian at Eden Hall Upper Elementary School in the Pine-Richland School District, Gibsonia, Pennsylvania, where she also serves as the library department chairperson and a building-level technology coach. She has been a school librarian in western Pennsylvania for eighteen years.

Strategic and Intentional

"The principal's mission isn't about preservation of 'the library'
but about creating the best spaces for students to learn and to
showcase the best of our students."

—*Carolyn Foote*

The school principal will not embrace the unique role of the librarian unless they are convinced of the impact of the program as a whole. It's not about having a librarian or even a library space—it's about how the librarian leads what happens in that space, and about what is impacted by the librarian outside of the space. School librarians need to employ strategies that help principals understand that role.

One of the most effective ways to cultivate that understanding is simply to listen and observe. Every district communication or building meeting can be an opportunity for librarians to showcase the value of the school library. Advocacy is not just about telling others what you have done. It's about demonstrating to others how the goals of your program can align with their goals. School librarians must actively endeavor to understand their principal's interests, needs, and priorities on both a personal and professional level. Librarians should be well versed in the strategic initiatives of the building and district and be able to articulate where these initiatives and the goals of the library program intersect. One-way school librarians can show this alignment is to develop a library mission statement that meets these criteria. Developing such a statement with the principal and leadership team is an even stronger indication of the contribution of the library to the learning community.

School librarians should be proactive and intentional about communicating with all stakeholders, but especially with principals. Through observation and everyday interactions, school librarians can determine their principal's communication preferences. Then, when we communicate with them, we can adapt our delivery to suit our principal. As part of the library operations plan, school librarians can be intentional about what to communicate and how often that communication should happen.

Understanding the principal's communication style is the first step in building a collaborative team for effective sharing of information. Librarians can be viewed as a positive distraction to principals when both have set expectations for how communication should happen. There are building leaders who prefer e-mail communication versus others who prefer a note in their mailbox or a drop-in face-to-face dialogue. Creating a collaborative team between the principal and librarian may prompt the librarian to ask, "How do you want to communicate with me?" Team development requires the pair to clarify communication styles in order to position the librarian as an asset to the school leader before a problem arises and communication is out of necessity.

After learning the principal's preferred mode of communication, librarians should create a plan to share the details of the library program before being asked. Librarians may view this as advocacy efforts, but to the principal this is called "managing upward" (Rousmaniere 2015). This communication plan should highlight how the school library is helping classroom teachers and students achieve academic success with building or district-level goals. Understanding that the principal's time is in high demand, librarians should strive to communicate as concisely as possible. (A photo, video, or link might have more impact than an essay.) When we are proactive with this communication, principals can trust they are up to date with the most current data and trends.

When an opportunity arises for a face-to-face conversation with the principal, librarians should be vigilant about checking on the principal's needs. Debra Kachel says, "Instead of telling the principal what's happening, ask the principal what he or she wants to happen." Kachel goes on to write: "Is the SLP (school library program) helping to achieve building goals? How can the SLP do a better job? This changes the conversation to become more collaborative, engaging, and productive, allowing the librarian to learn helpful insights into the principal's priorities" (Kachel 2017, 51).

Commitment to Shared Leadership

Effective school leaders ask themselves, "What does my faculty need from me within the educational setting? What should I be learning in order to connect the school's learning experiences?" This is an opportunity to showcase the leader as a learner while advancing strategic planning initiatives.

The follow-up questions steer the leader toward visible and responsive actions for building capacity and change. "Who can guide me to professional learning communities relevant to my area of new learning? Who curates the high-quality resources available to educators within our school environment?"

Principals answer these questions by studying the people and resources available to them. The school librarian can answer these questions and point principals in the direction of school improvement through a collaborative relationship. The guiding principles of this relationship must be reciprocal.

Joel Hoag, principal at Freedom Intermediate School, recognizes the value of a commitment to the inclusion of a school librarian as a learning partner and creator of curriculum: "It's been wonderful to have a framework that lets me see how we want to take learning from surface level and take it all the way through to application and content creation" (AASL 2020).

Principals extend the reach of the librarian by studying the competing factors for school priorities. The analysis of the school budget and allocation of resources serve as monthly tactical check-ins for the collaborative partnership. It should not occur as the annual budget proposal process in isolation from the ongoing needs of the school community. The monthly check-in is an integral part of empowering the librarian to share ideas and explore opportunities to showcase adult and student learning.

Building-level budgetary decisions can have a ripple effect on librarians and the work they can do. Before principals can advocate for the role of the librarian, they need to have a deep understanding of the role and the broader community impacted by their influence. Advocacy is about sharing the narrative in an authentic way. In order to tell their stories about establishing environments sparking students to innovate and create, leaders need to dedicate time to observe and participate in the daily library operations. Principals can advocate for the people and resources if time is dedicated to learning about the space and curation of the resources within the librarian's daily role. School-wide collaboration can be promoted if the principal and librarian model this engagement situated within the context of constructing a schedule and supportive services aligned to the strategic planning goals of the building.

VIGNETTE: IN-DEPTH PROGRAM REVIEW (IDPR): "LOOK FOR THE OPPORTUNITIES"

Kelly Gustafson

During the 2019–2020 school year, our K–12 library and English Language Arts (ELA) departments were two areas of focus in our district's cycle for In-Depth Program Review (IDPR). Each month, department representatives met to investigate and prioritize strengths, opportunities, action steps, and recommendations. The library team researched exemplar practices, connected with experts in the field, and engaged in civil discourse around the foundation of our findings and ideas for implementation. Our intent was to inform our current library program through the systematic process aligned to a larger strategic plan. This process felt messy and uncomfortable at times. Brian Miller, our superintendent, along with the Senior Leadership Team members, served as coaches throughout the monthly meetings, checking in and reminding the K–12 librarians to trust the process. I learned to step back and let the team of experts engage in the exchange of ideas.

During the nine-month review process, the role of a school librarian became further defined for me. The scope of their leadership role within a school and across curricular areas is more dynamic than I had realized in my instructional leadership practices. I questioned how I could increase the visibility of the impact they have on student learning by sharing my IDPR experiences with my administrative colleagues. If this idea were to happen, the library and ELA teams would no longer meet in the same professional development room while doing research as a parallel cohort. Ideally, they would be seated at the table beside each other, designing and curating resources to support lessons and innovation.

I relied on Beth Shenefiel, the academic leadership chair for library, to filter my advocacy ideas through a librarian lens. She helped me study my priorities by grounding my data sources and teaching me ways to monitor growth and the organization of learning within my building. I knew the ripple effect of our decisions through the continuous improvement process would begin as soon as we articulated the new Pine-Richland Library Department philosophy and vision to internal and external stakeholders. My responsiveness to the adjustments and challenges in our team's decision-making process reflected Tuckman's five stages of team development (forming, storming, norming, performing, and adjourning) (Wilson 2017).

The success of the library team's IDPR reflects the relationships built during the project with their combined abilities. Each member had to fully commit to the department philosophy and vision before our collaboration evolved into the fourth stage of team development: Performing. Superintendent Miller's open communication with me and Beth empowered us to confidently articulate the essential components needed to build a strong library program. I found myself scheduling frequent meetings with Beth to ask for assistance with new ideas and ways to lead other curricular areas. I always felt the need to share what I had gained from Beth with my colleagues.

At the time, I didn't realize how fast the ripple effect of our work was spreading among other principals. Beth and I worked in tandem to understand how to incorporate the philosophy and vision image and words into an advocacy plan reinforcing the concept of the library as a hub of learning in the schools. Using an iterative process to gain input by listening to each other and reflecting on our research, the team agreed on the vision graphic (see Figure 6.1) and philosophy statement: "Sparking curiosity, creating connections, empowering learners." This was evidence of the norming stage of Tuckman's team development (Wilson 2017).

Each IDPR meeting's agenda offered time for our team to make connections and recommendations around our respective areas of research. As we sat in the large conference room, I didn't think to connect us to the ELA educators and principals sitting across the same room. Perhaps it was too early to make the intentional connection between the two teams as we were still strengthening our alignment from within our own teams. I wondered if I had missed the opportunity to align administrators with the library team and their areas of expertise. During the presentation of our IDPR to internal and external stakeholders, I witnessed the support and authenticity of the value that our school community places on the role of school librarians and programming. This meant that there would be opportunities to make stronger connections during the second year of IDPR.

One of the emerging recommendations from the ELA team centered around social justice, inclusive practices, and diversity. I saw this as an opportunity to get a seat at the table for our K–12 librarians. The strategic move to include the professionals who read widely with graduate-level research skills would become another positive ripple effect within the district. I could not let this become a missed opportunity in my advocacy efforts. Instructional leaders build capacity in their development of strong teams.

Figure 6.1 Pine-Richland School District vision.

Two months after the presentation of our findings and recommendations to the Pine-Richland school directors, Jacob Missinger, our middle school assistant principal, reached out to me to discuss the action steps targeted by the ELA team. His inquiry centered around the need for expertise in diverse literature collections and social justice awareness.

My immediate response was: "You need to call Beth Shenefiel. She taught me everything I know!" The table was set, and Beth's chair was pulled out for her expertise. Jacob was about to experience what has shaped the key drivers in making instructional decisions as a principal. Tuckman's (Wilson 2017) team development stages were beginning again but with members forming a new collaborative team to promote diversity within literature resources.

I am most effective, as an instructional leader, when I distribute leadership among the team of educators who have specialized skill sets to merge best practices with innovation. Empowering Beth and the library team to balance critical thinking and mining for conflict when making decisions that will ultimately impact student learning is the basis of building capacity in a distributive leadership culture. Jacob's passion for leading social justice change was complemented by Beth's pedagogy rooted in AASL standards and the cross-cutting ELA standards. This marriage of strategic thinking will lead our library and ELA teams through the development of our IDPR action plans together.

Kelly (she/her) is the principal at Wexford Elementary School in the Pine-Richland School District, Gibsonia, Pennsylvania. Kelly began her career as a special education teacher. After pursuing graduate studies, she found her niche in educational leadership. She has served students, staff, and families for more than thirty years.

Your Principal, Your Ally

It has long been known that "principal advocacy is key to the development of a strong library media program that supports and enhances teaching and learning" (Haycock 1989, 10). The principal is the school librarian's most influential stakeholder. Librarians must be willing to step out of the comfort of our space and take the initiative to understand the needs of our students, colleagues, administrators, and community. We need to be willing to assume responsibility for leadership roles within our schools. We need to have the courage to speak up and take action to do what's best for each individual student.

Principals can demonstrate commitment to the librarian as a leader within the school community by providing opportunities that allow the librarian to utilize their unique skill set. They need to set high expectations for the librarians and library programs. Their commitment to library programs will be evidenced through word and action as they support the library through budgetary decisions, scheduling, and the promotion of collaborative instruction. When the librarian-principal alliance is strong, built on trust, and with the mutual understanding of the roles and responsibilities of the other, the school librarian and library program will be in a position to exert a positive influence on the school community.

Reflection Questions

1. How does your library program support the strategic goals of the building and district?
2. What opportunities exist for you to be a leader within your building and district?
3. How does a communication plan demonstrate your efforts to collaborate with the principal as an ally?

References

American Association of School Librarians. 2020. "Administrators on #AASL-standards." *YouTube* (video), June 26. Available at https://youtu.be/aMh THOM6kNo. Accessed October 1, 2020.

Bendekovic, David. 2020. Pennsylvania School Library Association. Grove City, PA.

Christfort, Kim, and Suzanne Vickberg. 2018. *Business Chemistry: Practical Magic for Crafting Powerful Work Relationships.* Hoboken, NJ: Wiley.

Church, Audrey P. 2008. "The Instructional Role of the Library Media Specialist as Perceived by Elementary School Principals." *School Library Media Research* 11. Available at http://www.ala.org/aasl/sites/ala.org.aasl/files /content/aaslpubsandjournals/slr/vol11/SLMR_InstructionalRole_V11.pdf. Accessed October 1, 2020.

Foote, Carolyn. 2015. "The Librarian—Principal Relationship." *Teacher Librarian* 42(4): 27–28.

Habley, Jennifer. 2019. "AASL Selects Seven School Administrators to Serve on Its School Leader Collaborative." *ALA News*, August 22. Available at http://www.ala.org/news/member-news/2019/08/aasl-selects-seven -school-administrators-serve-its-school-leader-collaborative. Accessed October 1, 2020.

Hartzell, Gary. 2007. "How Do Decision-Makers Become Library Media Advo-cates?" *Knowledge Quest* 36(1): 32–35.

Haycock, Ken. 1989. "Summary of EL Research Findings to Date: What Works, Research: The Implications for Professional Practice." Vancouver, BC: *Emergency Librarian*. Available at https://eric.ed.gov/?id=ED327181. Accessed October 1, 2020.

Kachel, Debra. 2017. "The Principal and the Librarian: Positioning the School Library Program." *Teacher Librarian* 45(1): 50–52.

Miller, Brian R. 2020. (Superintendent, Pine-Richland School District) in discus-sion with the author. August.

Pine-Richland School District. 2020. *PRSD Mission Vision and Values.* Available at
https://www.pinerichland.org/Page/8482. Accessed October 1, 2020.

Rousmaniere, Dana. 2015. "What Everyone Should Know about Managing Up."
Harvard Business Review 23. Available at https://hbr.org/2015/01/what
-everyone-should-know-about-managing-up.

Scholastic. 2016. *School Libraries Work! A Compendium of Research Supporting the
Effectiveness of School Libraries.* Available at https://www.scholastic.com
/SLW2016/resources/documents/SLW_Booklet_Final_Lo.pdf. Accessed
October 1, 2020.

Wilson, Carol. 2017. "Bruce Tuckman's Forming, Storming, Norming, & Performing Team Development Model." *Culture at Work.* Available at http://www
.coachingcultureatwork.com/bruce-tuckmans-forming-storming-norming
-performing-team-development-model. Accessed October 1, 2020.

CHAPTER 7

Leadership

Pam Harland and Anita Cellucci

Leadership requires confidence and vulnerability.

Leading from Our Passion and Purpose

As school librarians, we are often a singleton in our schools. Finding like-minded educators is essential to our professional growth and continued passion within our profession. When we, Pam and Anita, first met at ALA's annual conference at an AASL Affiliate Assembly meeting, we immediately discussed our ideas, shared stories, and felt a kinship over our careers, plans, and passions. We became friends at that conference while sharing meals and late-night drinks in the hotel restaurant. There is something about being exhausted at the end of the school year, traveling to a conference, attending a full schedule of meetings, staying up all night talking, and being surrounded by passionate librarians that filled us with energy and excitement. This shared experience is what brought us together. We both came from a place of authenticity, openness, risk taking, and confidence in our work and in our lives.

Since that first meeting, we have both served on AASL's Board of Directors in the same position, but at different times. We work together today educating future school librarians with a focus on leadership. The school librarian preparation program at Plymouth State University is based on the foundational belief that school librarians are essential, integral, and transformational leaders. We believe that school librarians are the catalysts for school change and organizational learning and will serve as leaders in their schools in areas of social justice, digital equity, social-emotional learning, cultural responsiveness, and positive school culture.

> *"When I dare to be powerful, to use my strength in the service of my vision, then it becomes less and less important whether I am afraid."*
>
> —Audre Lorde

Vulnerability is at the core of who we are as educators, integral to our continued friendship, and important in our work together. We support each other's ideas, speaking honestly from the heart. We are resolutely building a community of school librarians who are leading the way by holding space for each other and honoring each other's individual truth. Together, we push each other to dream of new ideas that support our communities of learners. Sharing an understanding of power is a gift that helps build our confidence— together. Our current passions and purpose create the foundation for this chapter. We are both interested in creating a community of school librarians who are prepared to be leaders in their schools by sharing practical ways we can model our values and increase our capacity to lead.

Understanding School Librarian Leadership

In their proposed theory of school librarian leadership, Everhart and Johnston (2016) defined school librarian leadership as "the ability to influence and inspire others to meet identified goals or to share an identified vision" (2). We work with our school communities to improve student learning and school culture, and help connect students and educators with the information and tools they need to succeed. Mendenhall (2013) stated that school librarians serve as change agents in their schools as they are "in a position to have a broad impact with their ideas and to foster the agility, innovation, and rapid learning capacity crucial to . . . survival and success" (183). Working collaboratively, school librarian leaders integrate instruction into content areas across the curriculum and grade levels to create a meaningful learning environment dedicated to helping students become information literate and successful lifelong learners.

> *"Sane leadership is developing the capacity to observe what's going on in the whole system and then either reflect that back or bring people together to consider where we are now."*
>
> —Margaret J. Wheatley

School librarian leadership is the ability to influence the school community on the access and use of information and resources to meet the needs and values of the school for the sake of improving the quality of learning for all. In addition, one of our underlying goals is to build a community of learners by cultivating belonging. Borkoski states, "There is consensus in the literature about the benefits of a student's sense of belonging. Researchers suggest that higher levels of belonging lead to increases in GPA, academic achievement, and motivation" (2019, 30). Leadership from the library allows us to demonstrate this idea in a number of ways, as depicted in the vignettes we share later in this chapter. In order to accomplish this, we believe school librarians need to incorporate into our practice both confidence and vulnerability. This updated definition details the complex social processes that make up school librarian leadership.

Questions for School Librarian Leaders

1. How do you demonstrate leadership in your daily practice?
2. How do you influence your school culture without the authority of a traditional school leader?
3. In what ways do you improve the quality of learning for all?
4. How do you cultivate a sense of belonging for students at your school?
5. Who are the leaders you have most admired, and what behaviors and attitudes do or did they exhibit?

Confidence to Lead

Everhart and Johnston (2016) define confidence using the Oxford Dictionary definition, "A feeling of self-assurance arising from one's appreciation of one's own abilities or qualities" (Oxford University Press 2018). With confidence, a school librarian is able to create positive relationships, effectively communicate, and develop collaborative activities across the school community. Each of these activities contributes toward a librarian's ability to lead.

One way in which school librarians demonstrate confidence is through the collaborative integration of technology into the school's curriculum. Through this process, we are able to share our expertise in curriculum, our understanding of technological tools and services, and our pedagogical knowledge. "These opportunities for leadership are vital in providing school librarians with the experience, confidence, and skills necessary for leadership involvement" (Johnston 2012, 18). When we show our expertise in areas others know little about, classroom teachers and administrators will see us as leaders.

Experience and education further contribute to a librarian's confidence. School librarians who demonstrate confidence have access to the resources that meet curricular needs as well as the knowledge and skills to succeed in their positions. In the research on transforming school librarians to leaders, Baker states, "Having the right tools, as well as the knowledge and skills to integrate those tools effectively, gives people the confidence to get their job done" (2016, 147). An understanding of innovative technological tools and collaborative instruction as well as experience with a variety of information resources can be gained through professional learning, such as school librarian preparation programs, workshops, webinars, and conferences. With practice comes expertise and, subsequently, confidence.

> *"Because they trust themselves . . . they have no need to convince*
> *others by deception. Since their confidence has never deteriorated,*
> *they need not be fearful of others."*
>
> —Chögyam Trungpa

School librarians who demonstrate confidence have the resources, knowledge, and skills to succeed in their positions as well as internal trust in themselves. For school librarians, demonstrating confidence shows an understanding of a school librarian leader's professional identity. School librarians with confidence believe we can run an effective school library because we have curated the resources we need to do our job. We have the preparation, the desire, and the experience to apply tools and resources in classroom-library collaborative instruction. Confidence is built out of intentional preparation and self-reflection. It is a belief in our own ability, skills, and experience.

As librarians, it is essential that we continuously look for ways to move forward by consistent, thoughtful, and intentional practice. "As you think about your own path to daring leadership, remember Joseph Campbell's wisdom: 'The cave you fear to enter holds the treasure you seek.' Own the fear, find the cave, and write a new ending for yourself, for the people you're meant to serve and support, and for your culture. Choose courage over comfort. Choose whole hearts over armor. And choose the great adventure of being brave and afraid. At the exact same time" (Brown 2018, 272).

In schools, change often involves new pedagogy, student issues, or schoolwide initiatives such as new curricula or policies. The secret to overcoming resistance to change is to embrace the idea that we can actually help support a shift within our school and community by making the student, teacher, or administrator the priority. When we pause to think about the feelings that the person is experiencing and offer suggestions on the spot to manage the change, we can often facilitate that shift. If we view each interaction with compassion, the flow naturally begins. This takes confidence to start, and once we have the support of the school community, our confidence grows exponentially.

The Strength of Vulnerability

Vulnerability is defined by Dr. Brené Brown as the demonstration of "uncertainty, risk, and emotional exposure" (2012, 34). Our research and experience show that librarian leaders who have confidence in their role are willing to share their vulnerability. They demonstrate this by:

- Including other perspectives in decisions (giving voice to the voiceless).
- Openly sharing that they may not know everything but they know where to find information.
- Taking risks to increase access and innovate.
- Sharing emotions with colleagues through the development of deep and caring relationships.

A school library is at the center of the school often physically but invariably, metaphorically. School librarians must firmly believe that community building can transform the way in which a school is able to tackle issues related to teaching and learning. With this belief, we can play an important role. Historically, a community has been based on a location, a place where people lived. It is now more commonly recognized as a group of like-minded people with common goals and understandings. The Oxford Dictionary (2020) has several definitions for community, and the one that most closely resembles mainstream understanding reads: "a feeling of fellowship with others, as a result of sharing common attitudes, interests, and goals."

As we seek to fulfill our purpose as connectors and collaborators, it is important for us to first consider the culture of our schools. Trust must be present in the relationships before an effective collaboration can take place. In order to build trust, each person must be willing to be vulnerable. Showing vulnerability can be a very uncomfortable place, and moving through this takes finesse, patience, and intentional practice.

> *"Vulnerability is the birthplace of innovation, creativity, and change"*
> *and "to create is to make something that has never existed before.*
> *There's nothing more vulnerable than that."*
>
> —*Brené Brown*

If we think of vulnerability in this way, we are able to push through discomfort to bring about our ability to create change. To get to the trust, we must be vulnerable and nonjudgmental of each other.

Commitment to Leadership

Commitment in terms of leadership is taking responsibility and being accountable for one's intentions and actions to influence the values and behaviors of others toward more positive, effective outcomes for all members of the learning community. Intentional planning, relationship building, and continuous learning about educational strategies and ideas are important to committing to the work of a librarian leader. Being intentional in planning diverse programming creates a pathway to fill the gaps within a school culture and leads to instilling a sense of belonging for our students. When a school librarian understands the challenges confronting the community, has intentionally built relationships, and is willing to listen authentically, there is an opportunity to cocreate a more positive culture within a school.

Making the commitment to leadership is to rise to the challenge of classroom-library collaboration for instruction. If school librarians do not influence classroom teaching in the many ways needed (i.e., relevant, culturally responsive teaching and student-driven learning), then we have not reached our capacity to lead. We understand that this is challenging, especially when we are new in a school librarian role or during administrative changes, but developing these instructional partnerships will benefit students, teachers, and our role as a school librarian leader.

Leadership is about developing trust and having the tough conversations that strengthen the community of learners. Relationship building should begin with the school principal. Ensuring that the principal not only understands how a school librarian is integral to school culture but also how we are able to collaborate with teachers in creating learning environments and instruction to support improved student learning outcomes.

In order to have influence, school librarians must not only follow through on our promises to other educators, but also be willing to be humble and meet classroom teachers where they are and begin from there. As the great educational reformer bell hooks writes, the practice of teaching and learning comes easiest to those of us "who believe that our work is not merely to share information but to share in the intellectual and spiritual growth of our students" (1994, 13). School librarians demonstrate this, and as leaders in our schools we are empowered to create a positive culture of both intellectual and emotional growth for all our students.

Questions for School Librarian Leaders

1. How do you build trust with colleagues and students?
2. Where did your confidence as a school librarian leader come from?
3. How do you feel about sharing vulnerability with colleagues and students?
4. What are the values, intentions, and behaviors that describe who you want to be as a school librarian leader?

The Courage to Lead

School librarians demonstrate the courage to lead through our attitudes, decisions, and actions. School librarian leaders who incorporate confidence and vulnerability into our practice are able to develop innovative ideas by listening to the entire school community. We intentionally build close and trusting relationships with staff and students through collaborative teaching efforts and open communication. Additionally, we advocate for stakeholders who are not always represented when making decisions. As leaders, we have trust in ourselves and are not afraid to speak up when an injustice or need is recognized.

We have included two vignettes of school librarian leaders who illustrate confidence and vulnerability in their practice. Although both of these librarians serve at the high school level, their experiences and behaviors can apply to school librarians at all levels. Envisioning a community-centered library in order to more readily develop belonging is at the core of their practice, and that, in turn, has helped develop school cultures that support the work of these librarians.

VIGNETTE: VULNERABILITY IS OUR SUPERPOWER

Iris Eichenlaub

I see myself as the steward of our co-constructed, community-centered library. As a leader in my school, I have come to recognize that some of my greatest influence is because I am comfortable being vulnerable. This vulnerability is also tied to feeling confident in who I am as a professional and as a valued member of my school community. I see our library as a place of engagement for students and staff, and intentionally invite their participation so that being in the space itself becomes an action that brings life to our library.

I inherited a traditional library that had fallen out of use and was sadly closed most of the time. My first order of business was to hear the voices of the school community, so I created a student advisory board, surveyed students, spent time talking with faculty and staff, and volunteered to serve on a variety of school and district teams. What did this community need from their library? I listened to what the stakeholders had to say, took a seat at the table, and began serving as the agent of change in my school—from the library.

I initially began by working with the administration and facilities department on rearranging and refurbishing the library space in order to permit food and drinks, as it was a top request from our students. Additionally, I cultivated a welcoming, safe space where students and staff could come for help on almost anything. Informed by the input of what my community needed, I expanded the boundaries of the role of our library and how it could be a responsive and dynamic space.

Co-Constructed Space

When freshmen first come into the library for orientation in the fall, I start off by saying, "Some of the best parts of this library are because of your great ideas, so please share them" (Eichenlaub 2018). The library is a dynamic, living space, a space that the community co-constructs together, and a space that responds to the needs of the community. Because I strive to make connections between people and ideas, I am open to sharing new recommendations, especially on behalf of those individuals who do not necessarily possess the formal power to make and implement decisions.

Creating a co-constructed space with students also creates a sense of well-being, as students are made to feel comfortable sharing ideas, and they have an understanding and a voice in the decisions made about the library. Seeing the library as a communal space ensures that everyone contributes toward this learning community. I think of myself as the steward of the library: working to implement and respond to the changing needs of the community; iterating and adapting as new ideas, issues, and opportunities arise. Will the library always look and be the same from year to year? Not if I'm doing my job properly!

> *"Rather than thinking about vulnerability as a weakness,*
> *I see it as a superpower."*
>
> —*Iris Eichenlaub*

Vulnerability is closely tied to understanding who I am, what my strengths and challenges are, and feeling comfortable and valued in my work environment. I'm confident as a professional, but I will also tell you when I am stumped, and I will absolutely not ever pretend that I know more than I do. When I let teachers, students, parents, or administrators know that I am unsure about a problem or solution, I'm demonstrating vulnerability, authenticity, and integrity. It's this transparency that engenders trust with my colleagues because they know that I will ultimately follow through with them.

The position school librarians are in allows us to see from a whole-school perspective. I am willing to share uncertainty that leads to being open to additional perspectives and subsequently allows for a greater inclusion of ideas in order to improve the entire school community. My courage to be vulnerable is demonstrated by freely admitting that I do not know the answer to every technology challenge or information search, but I am willing, capable, and eager to find the answer and solution.

As a librarian, I include human resources in my mental Rolodex when I am looking for possible solutions. My natural tendency is to think about who in my school or broader community might have experience with the problem I'm facing. When a colleague approaches me with a technology issue, I start by thinking about who in our building might have encountered something similar. What seemed so easy to me—reaching out to others for help—was actually quite novel in my building, which had a pretty typical, siloed high school culture. So, my cheerful suggestions to find help from a colleague was initially considered a radical act of modeling confidence in vulnerability. This kind of cross-pollination began to foster connections within our previously siloed school culture, where it was scary to let your colleagues see you in a vulnerable space. The collective professional learning is amplified when teachers can be vulnerable with each other and learn from one another.

Building Trust

When teachers need help from me, they are being vulnerable, so building trusting relationships is paramount. I learned early on, especially with technology questions, that when teachers are in the role of learners, a lot of those old learner tapes start playing. I often think that the adult person who is presenting to me is giving me a little window into how they were as a little person. Frequently, the teacher is coming to me frustrated that they couldn't solve their own problem or anxious that their class starts in 5 minutes and something isn't right with the technology they had planned on using. Sometimes a teacher is irritable and ashamed. How would you respond if this were a child in front of you? We can't get to a problem-solving mind-set when we haven't addressed the teacher's emotional needs first—just like with our students. So, my first step is always to validate that teacher's emotions and help them calm down so we can activate the other hemisphere of their brain. Patience and kindness go a long way, and it's much easier to find solutions together when a teacher feels calmly supported. Understanding emotional exposure plays a part in the vulnerability that school leaders demonstrate.

I don't mind having my technology flop in front of a class or my colleagues, but I don't like getting it wrong when it comes to relationships or how I handled an interaction with a student or colleague. It's usually when I am on my commute home at the end of the day, as my thoughts about the day unspool, that I realize that I have missed an opportunity for connection, spoke too sharply, was impatient, and the like. Learning how to apologize and rebuild that trust is another way I have worked to cultivate my vulnerability. Especially with students, this has a big impact; an adult apologizing to a child is a rare event. My ability to do well at my work depends on my community's trust in me. Building and maintaining trust is at the center of what I do as a leader in our library and in my school.

Iris Eichenlaub is the librarian/technology integrator at Camden Hills Regional High School in Rockport, Maine. She is the 2017 Knox County Teacher of the Year and was named an Inspiring Educator in 2017 by the Maine Education Association. Iris serves on the board of the Maine Association of School Libraries and has served as a Knowledge Quest *blogger.*

VIGNETTE: THE SOUL OF A LIBRARIAN: CONFIDENCE, COMPASSION, COMMUNITY

Anita Cellucci

I have always seen my role as a school librarian as a passion project. That is to say, I bring passion, energy, and love to cultivate an authentic space in the library where the community feels welcomed, seen, and celebrated. When I focus my attention on what I value most, I am able to use both confidence and vulnerability in my practice.

"When soul is present in education, attention shifts. As the quality of attention shifts, we listen with great care not only to what people say but to the messages between the words—tones, gestures, the flicker of feeling across the face. And then we concentrate on what has heart and meaning."

—Rachael Kessler

This quote by Rachael Kessler from her book *The Soul of Education: Helping Students Find Connection, Compassion, and Character at School* (2000) speaks to the core of my vision as a school librarian. My work as a librarian is to create an authentically compassionate space. The root of this for me is very personal. As a child, the public library was the place where I was able to let go of anxiety and settle into a story. I often chose stories that were steeped in empathy as a way to see a hopeful pathway through my own life. In a sense, as a school librarian, I want to create exactly what I needed as a child. I know that schools are filled with youth who need to be listened to and need to have a space that allows them to speak their truth (Kessler 2000).

Focusing on the soul of the library allows compassion to grow and flourish in all areas. The curriculum becomes more inclusive, the space more welcoming, and the librarian the heart. My purpose has been something I have spent a large amount of time reflecting on. For me, it's an exercise in grounding, especially in those moments when I ask myself if I am on the right path. Creating opportunity for those who feel voiceless to implement their ideas, afraid to find their passion, or are unsure of how to feel at peace with who they truly are as a person has long been important to my personal and professional growth. This is the central reason I became a school librarian and why I continue to accept leadership roles. Confidence has been a journey of self-reflection, and remaining vulnerable to my administrators, colleagues, and students has had a major impact on my ability to be a leader and to foster an inclusive community.

Practicing Vulnerability

Several years ago, my position as a middle school librarian was reduced to part-time due to financial challenges within the district. I was incredibly shocked, as my program was based on inquiry and student learning. This experience, although heart wrenching, was also enlightening. Schools are a bureaucratic system that force educators to be strategic in how their mission is envisioned and enacted. I realized that understanding the community is essential to gaining support from administration and other educators. I had been focusing solely on providing a solid library program. This change in perception allowed me to focus on building trusting relationships with the entire school community.

In my next position as a high school librarian, I vowed to enact leadership differently. I strategically planned the program I envisioned and collaborated with all stakeholders on its development. The framework of the program needed transparency, visibility, and ownership beyond the school library. This was a scary undertaking and left me feeling vulnerable, but I kept my passion for creating an inclusive library at the forefront of our plan.

Today vulnerability has a permanent and prominent place in everything I do. Knowing that I can lean into the intentionality of our collaborative plan allows me to act with confidence. Moving in the direction of a student-driven learning space involves risks, but they are necessary. Showing vulnerability is a way to develop relationships with the entire school community. I need to be the one who is willing to take a risk. As Brené Brown urges us to do, "step into the arena . . . I want to be brave with my life. And when we make the choice to dare greatly, we sign up to get our asses kicked. We can choose courage or we can choose comfort, but we can't have both. Not at the same time" (Brown 2015, 4).

Culturally Responsive Programming

I have often reflected on my own challenging childhood experiences as a way to understand the potential of the school librarian. Now as an educator trained in how trauma, mental health, and adverse childhood experiences play an integral role in how our students are able to engage at school, I know I need to bring culturally responsive strategies into my teaching. A grounding aspect of being culturally responsive is the act of relationship building with students. The library needs to not only be a place where students feel comfortable but more so a community space where they feel ownership. In our library, this has manifested into programs that are youth-led, sustainable, and provide a space to grow equity.

One initiative is Poetry Power. A poetry group is an impactful way to hold space for youth, respect their voices, and provide opportunities to amplify their creativity. A poetry community offers a safe space for students to engage in informed conversation and active debate, interact with other learners who reflect a range of perspectives, and reflect on their own place within the global learning community. Students find freedom in this after-school club through a focus on diverse voices that allows them to widen the spectrum of their ideas, thoughts, and writing. Often the conversation and the space to be heard is the most important aspect of the group.

A pivotal focus in our library has been mental health. Several years ago, the statistics from our district's mental health survey were changing alarmingly. Students were reporting a higher percentage of suicidal ideation, anxiety, and feelings of depression. I could see this gap in our school culture's response to this situation and could also envision the school library as a solution. A federal grant helped me develop educational programming for staff and students that focused on creating a stigma-free environment where students could learn, share, and find support for mental wellness. I felt strongly that educators did not have the training to identify a student in crisis. I worked with the public library and town youth and family services to certify teachers in the district for Youth Mental Health First Aid to help them understand their role.

As a way to integrate student involvement and increase mental wellness into the learning environment, we started a student wellness advisory, and I developed a curriculum for bibliotherapy. Mind Matters, a student-led advisory, is made possible through a grant from the Shine Initiative. The goal of the advisory is to implement initiatives that both support the mental health of the students and instill a greater understanding of mental wellness throughout the school. Bibliotherapy has been another important way to integrate cultural responsiveness and social justice awareness into my practice. Collaboration with counselors, clinicians, and English teachers has built a community that sees all students, even the most vulnerable, as readers and allows students to identify their strengths and challenges as a continuum instead of an end point. This initiative asks students to reflect on their identity as a reader and to develop a growth plan through collaboration between the librarian and their English teacher.

As the single school librarian in the building, often we are misunderstood in our role in creating positive school culture. Considering this a challenge instead of a stop sign has helped me to persevere through times when there was a lack of support. These initiatives have become an integral part of curriculum in classes, small groups, and the library space. These programs are examples of how I have led with my values and didn't stay silent about tough topics.

Anita Cellucci is the school librarian at Westborough High School, Westborough, Massachusetts. She advises a teen advisory and coaches a poetry spoken word team. For her work in social-emotional learning, she was named a 2019 LJ Mover & Shaker and received the SLJ & Scholastic School Librarian of the Year 2016 Award.

Leadership Matters

A school librarian leader is not an autonomous leader of a library program within the walls of the physical library. To lead and succeed, each individual member of the school must be an integrated component of the school's community and culture. Lance and Kachel (2018) explain that the school library impact studies "have often found that the benefits associated with good library programs are strongest for the most vulnerable and at-risk learners, including students of color, low-income students, and students with disabilities." A school librarian who has cultivated their commitment and purpose through the habits of mind of passion and courage will be well placed to be a leader as well as to impact student learning in a meaningful way.

"What didn't you do to bury me; but you forgot that I was a seed."

—*Dinos Christianopoulos*

School librarian leaders who give voice to the most vulnerable and work to push the boundaries of education as a path toward freedom can proudly stand by librarian values. When we do, we will expand both respect and trust throughout our school communities. We will be the leaders who plant the seeds in order to grow future leaders.

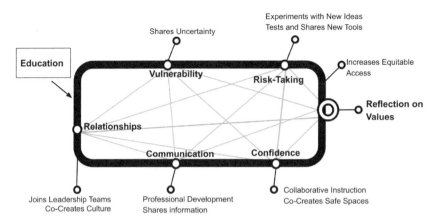

Figure 7.1 CVSL model of school librarian leadership behaviors (Harland 2019).

In Figure 7.1, we illustrate the interconnected behaviors of school librarian leaders.

The entry point onto the map indicated by "education" is the platform of a school librarian's education—formal and informal preparation. The stops along the map depict the behaviors and characteristics of the school librarian leader. Each stop is interconnected and eventually leads to all other behaviors. "Reflection on values" serves as a dynamic and transformational point that provides school librarian leaders with the opportunity to reflect on our own personal values and skills and those that align with the values and needs of the school. This point enables us to envision, plan, and implement a change process in order to improve equitable access to resources, tools, and instruction. This also creates an opening for attention to diversity, inclusion, and intellectual freedom for all library stakeholders.

Opportunities for school librarians to demonstrate leadership stem from each of the behavior points on this model of school librarian leadership behaviors. These points encourage several external outcomes of leadership, including joining leadership teams, offering professional development, and practicing collaborative instruction. Several points reflect internal outcomes stemming from the internal indicators of confidence and vulnerability. This model extends Everhart and Johnston's (2016) model of school librarian leadership with the inclusion of risk taking and vulnerability as well as the addition of opportunities.

School librarians build trusting relationships throughout the school community. We have direct knowledge of the entire school's curriculum and expertise in information resources and pedagogy, which places us in a position to take on a leadership role (Johnston 2015; Moreillon 2018). We also have the power to cultivate belonging for all of our students, specifically those students who may need that sense of community most. If we are to create the necessary environment for today's school librarians to successfully take on a leadership role, the development of an open, innovative, and collaborative culture and our own confidence and vulnerability are emerging imperatives.

Reflection Questions

1. How do you demonstrate vulnerability and confidence in your leadership practice?
2. What difference have you made/hope to make in your school culture as a school librarian leader?
3. What moments of leadership are you most proud of? What did those moments look and feel like? Who did those moments impact?

References

Baker, Sheila. 2016. "From Teacher to School Librarian Leader and Instructional Partner: A Proposed Transformation Framework for Educators of Preservice School Librarians." *School Libraries Worldwide* 22(1): 143–159.

Borkoski, Carey. 2019. "Cultivating Belonging." *Accessibility, Compliance, and EQUITY in Education*. November/December: 28–33.

Brown, Brené. 2012. *Daring Greatly: How the Courage to Be Vulnerable Transforms the Way We Live, Love, Parent, and Lead*. New York: Avery.

Brown, Brené. 2015. *Rising Strong: How the Ability to Reset Transforms the Way We Live, Love, Parent, and Lead*. New York: Random House.

Brown, Brené. 2018. *Dare to Lead*. New York: Avery.

Eichenlaub, Iris. 2018. "What's a Student-Centered Library?" *Knowledge Quest* (blog). Available at https://knowledgequest.aasl.org/whats-a-student -centered-library. Accessed October 1, 2020.

Everhart, Nancy, and Melissa P. Johnston. 2016. "A Proposed Theory of School Librarian Leadership: A Meta-Ethnographic Approach." *School Library Research* 19. Available at https://eric.ed.gov/?id=EJ1120868. Accessed October 1, 2020.

Harland, Pamela. 2019. "An Investigation into the Leadership Behaviors of School Librarian Leaders: A Qualitative Study." EdD dissertation, Plymouth State University.

hooks, bell. 1994. *Teaching to Transgress: Education as the Practice of Freedom*. London: Routledge.

Johnston, Melissa. 2012. "School Librarians as Technology Integration Leaders: Enablers and Barriers to Leadership Enactment." *School Library Research* 15. Available at http://www.ala.org/aasl/sites/ala.org.aasl/files/content/aaslpubs andjournals/slr/vol15/SLR_School_Librarians_as_Technology_Integration _Leaders_V15.pdf. Accessed October 22, 2020.

Johnston, Melissa. 2015. "Distributed Leadership Theory for Investigating Teacher Librarian Leadership." *School Libraries Worldwide* 21(2): 39–57.

Kessler, Rachel. 2000. *The Soul of Education: Helping Students Find Connection, Compassion, and Character at School.* Alexandria, VA: ASCD Publications.

Lance, Keith Curry, and Debra E. Kachel. 2018. "Why School Librarians Matter: What Years of Research Tell Us." *Phi Delta Kappan* 99(7): 15–20.

Mendenhall, Mark E., ed. 2013. *Global Leadership: Research, Practice, and Development.* 2nd ed. Routledge Global Human Resource Management Series. New York: Routledge.

Moreillon, Judi. 2018. *Maximizing School Librarian Leadership: Building Connections for Learning and Advocacy.* Chicago: American Library Association.

Oxford University Press. 2018. "Confidence. Def. 1.2." *Oxford Dictionaries.* Available at https://en.oxforddictionaries.com/definition/us/confidence. Accessed October 22, 2020.

Oxford University Press. 2020. "Community, Def. 2A." *Oxford Dictionaries.* Available at https://en.oxforddictionaries.com/definition/us/community. Accessed October 22, 2020.

CHAPTER 8

Advocacy

Kristin Fraga Sierra and TuesD Chambers

Advocacy involves effective communication and building partnerships.

A Passion for School Library Advocacy

Authors' Note: We are writing this chapter during a pandemic. Some school librarian positions are being eliminated. Other school librarians' work is being redirected to other instructional functions due to school closures and remote learning. For us, this indicates that our contributions to student learning and classroom teachers' teaching are as yet not understood or valued in many schools and districts. In this environment, one-way communications that are traditionally viewed as public relations are absolutely essential. If we don't advocate for library programs and our own positions, the future of state-certified school librarians is in serious jeopardy. If we fail to speak for ourselves, many more K–12 students, classroom teachers, administrators, and families will not realize the benefits of state-certified school librarian literacy leaders on their campuses. We cannot let that happen.

With the constant up-to-the-minute flow of information, individuals receive a continual tsunami of messages. Due to the sheer volume of voices competing to capture our attention, school librarians must be purposeful and specific if our message is to successfully target and reach the members of the intended audience. Keeping this at the forefront of thought is important for school librarians in effectively planning for disseminating information about the school library program. Spreading the message for stakeholders to advocate for the program is an essential activity for today's school librarian, particularly during school closures.

"Now is not the time to wait to be invited to participate in the future of education. School librarians must seize this moment of forced change and share their skills and knowledge. Our learners are depending on us."

—Cherity Pennington

In examples of successful advocacy, school librarians must begin with intention that connects the message with the recipient. Considering the audience's best and most convenient way to receive communication is paramount to getting messages out and creating the deepest, widest impact. Students will receive and respond to communication differently than their parents; classroom teachers and staff will receive and respond differently than the greater community. School administrators and other decision makers have their own "big picture lens" and will also receive and respond differently than the other groups. Structuring advocacy efforts around that knowledge can make all the difference between hitting the perfect note with the intended audience or falling flat and starting over again.

Unlike other academic departments in schools with multiple team members, the school library department tends to be made up of one dedicated professional, in some cases a few, who work toward the success of the library. The school library should be a learning hub of the school in which members of other departments witness and participate in library learning and programs. When this happens, this is a form of advocacy in and of itself, as teachers and staff become partners in the library program and natural advocates. When it doesn't, the work of the school library program may go unnoticed. When libraries go unnoticed, even if effective work is being done, funding and staffing are in danger. Strong advocacy work is absolutely necessary to the survival of the school library and is a core, undeniable element to the position of the school librarian.

In "Big Picture Advocacy: Making Fifteen Minutes Count," former school librarian and Vancouver Public Schools Teacher of the Year Mark Ray (2012) advises school librarians to create a "one-page executive summary," a document with "clear, concise and compelling" statements about what is going well in the school library: highlights, services, benefits, and an impactful student-centered story. Ray also advises having this document at the ready and to update it often to be used to inform administrators, classroom teachers, parents, and community members. His advice streamlines the process, simplifying the seemingly overwhelming job of advocacy. Opportunities for connecting with important (or potential) stakeholders tend to spring up at unexpected times. This preparation enables the school librarian to have compelling truths and data to share at a moment's notice. Figure 8.1 is an example created by Kristin to advocate for the Lincoln High School Library program in Tacoma, Washington.

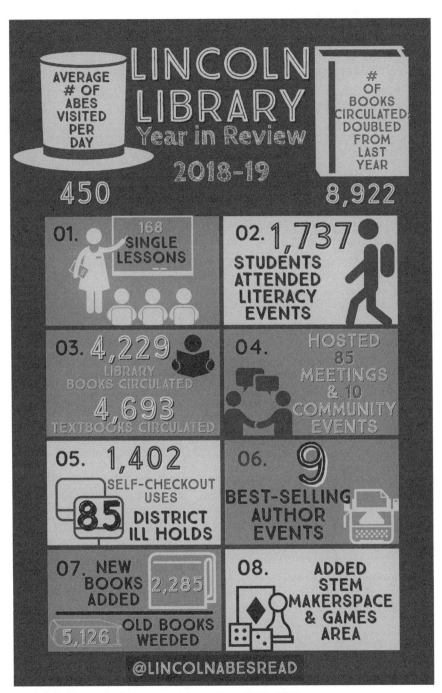

Figure 8.1 Lincoln Library year in review, 2018–2019.

In addition to creating a one-page summary, Ray advises the further step of memorizing the basics and to make the most of face-to-face time with others. "This is an opportunity to share the substance of school libraries— make it real for the listener" (2012, 31). Some call it a prepared "elevator speech," but more than that he purports that a 15-minute period is necessary to truly impress on listeners the impact of the school library by focusing on sharing work with students, successes, key ideas, and partnerships. Then, finish up with a "call to action" by suggesting ways the listener may become involved in furthering the success of the school library program.

Communicating with Students

Just as every classroom teacher must know their students well enough to choose the best strategy to teach them, so school librarians must learn the best ways to reach their students. The first and most necessary step to connecting with students is to get them in the library. To do this, the school librarian must take steps to offer programs, services, and materials, and develop strong working relationships and ongoing partnerships with classroom teachers. As with most professional responsibilities that require thought and preparation, library visits should include plenty of relevant "hooks" to involve students and classroom teachers in the library program.

School librarians must make direct and indirect invitations to join in a community and to benefit academically and socially from the library's services. These have the power to draw students in and keep them coming back. This may take shape in many forms:

- an invitation to participate in a future event or to join a club or program,
- a library brochure with hours, services, and contact information, or
- a bookmark or a magnet with links to the online catalog, the school library's website, the library's social media handles, and the librarian's contact information.

Students need to feel that they are a part of the library, that they are welcome, and that it is a place that can help them reach their goals and connect with what they need. Students need to know that the school library and the job of the librarian exist for them and their betterment. When this is conveyed successfully, students will respond.

School librarians ought to make every effort to try to think like their students, to put themselves "in their shoes." Balanced with what a school librarian knows is beneficial for students academically, this can be a recipe for connection with students. We can ask ourselves questions such as, "If I were a fourteen-year-old student, what are some of the pressures I would feel? What are some of the needs I may have?" Then, brainstorm ways we can structure the library schedule and services in order to meet those needs.

Using a marketing tool like a short student survey to get students' input allows them to use their voices to inform us as to what they look for and need in their school library. This is an effective way to be intentional in meeting students' needs. For example, the first year of high school can be an overwhelming year. Students are placed in bigger school environments; they may not know any peers or may not have maintained friendships from middle school. Many may feel lost and insecure, feeling the innate need to belong, and in need of a "home base" at school. The library can be that "home."

If the school librarian strives to create a warm, inviting place, accessible at key times—before the school day, lunch time, and after the school day—this could begin to meet those needs. And even better, during those times provide quality resources, clear systems, access to technology, mentors, tutors, and safe adults who offer individual support. That is a way for the school librarian to craft the library into a place and space that is truly student centered and vital to the lives of the students we serve.

I, Kristin, describe the power and significance of involving students in directing library programs, events, reading challenges, and activities in "Creating a Culture of Readers" (Sierra 2018). Like many librarians, I often find myself asking, "How can I effectively communicate what I have to offer and serve as many teachers and students as possible?" After surveying students and teachers, I formed a plan. For me in 2018, the answer came through an unexpected source—a tool I had been using for over a decade—Skype. In our middle school library, I worked with students and classroom teachers to dream big, reach out to relevant experts in their fields to inform and enrich student learning. This collaborative work resulted in bringing in dozens of professionals: authors, scientists, and special speakers virtually, and a few physically, into the school library and in front of our students.

Communicating with Classroom Teachers

School librarians are teachers. One more time for those in the back: school librarians are teachers. If there is one thing for certain, teachers have a greater impact when we work in tandem, when we help one another, and when we benefit from one another's strengths. When professionals combine our expertise for the benefit of students, there is transformative power in collaboration. When it comes to classroom teachers and school librarians working together, the benefits for students growing as learners and deepening community connections are only the tip of the iceberg.

"Advocating for things we believe in can be incredibly uncomfortable. . . .
If we don't step up, step out, and take steps, we may be ensuring
our own demise."

—Steve Tetreault

First and foremost, classroom teachers need to be convinced that although school librarians do not, in most cases, have classes assigned to us, we are in fact educators who have much to offer colleagues and students. School librarians must take the added step needed to establish relationships and systems of communication with classroom teachers. Library advocacy with teachers looks different from other groups since it is imperative to "advertise" how incorporating the school library and the expertise of the school librarian into their students' learning is going to both promote their classroom curriculum goals and support their students' growth in their content area.

When it comes to public relations directed to classroom teachers, its best to keep the message focused, succinct, and in brief format. Messages should help classroom teachers visualize working with the school librarian by providing actual examples of the past and potential partnerships that could be possible. Briefly share pictures or video and a short story of a successful and mutually beneficial coteaching experience. This could be accomplished in several ways. The best examples include a short e-mail with a few quick suggestions and links to more information and "the ask," a calendar invite for a brief meeting to discuss coteaching opportunities. Collaboration could start with a simple offer to visit the classroom in a support role or an offer to attend and possibly present at content-area or grade-level meetings for departments like English or social studies. If kept brief and relevant to each groups' specific and expressed needs, another example might be to present a content areas' professional development session or series with the focus on the resources, supports, and services provided by the school librarian.

"Future Ready librarians embrace change and innovation in education. As teachers, they empower students as creators and digital citizens; as coaches, they collaborate with teachers as curators and guides" (Ray cited in Vercelletto 2016). Classroom teachers have big jobs—jobs that require much planning, consistency, preparation, and patience. One of the pitfalls is its potential for isolation and burnout. Examples of successful and sustained partnerships offer hope to combat those pitfalls. And the more collegial support teachers receive, particularly the type of support that moves them along their professional goals while deepening and enriching their students' learning, the less teachers may experience feelings of being overwhelmed and fatigued. Relationships, connections, and a win-win situation for both parties can make all the difference.

Communicating with School Administrators

School administrators have the privilege of leading the entire school community, and with this they bear a heavy responsibility. As they say, "The buck stops here." Not only does "the buck" stop with them, but the literal "bucks" (dollars) assigned to schools are also distributed by administrators to all the departments in the school community. In many cases, and aside from district or federally mandated funds earmarked for specific students and programs, school administrators have leadership committees, advisory boards, and other school leaders to help them determine allocations based on needs and data. Chairs and members of these committees play a role in taking things off their school administrators' proverbial "plates" and can in many cases be mutually beneficial for the school library and the school librarian.

As a result, it behooves the school librarian to serve in one or more roles within the school leadership structure to have a say in planning and budgeting topics that affect the library. It is also a way to have a better, bigger picture of the inner workings of school leadership and the needs of the school community as a whole since the school librarian's job is to strive to meet the needs of the school community. Committee service is a very powerful way to show the impact of our service-focused leadership. Employing this kind of advocacy matters when the topic of where and how much money will be spent. Then, the school librarian quite literally has a seat at the table.

This might look different in different schools. In one school, it might be serving on the School-Centered Decision-Making (SCDM) committee, in another it might mean serving on the advisory board for the Associated Student Body (ASB) club and to guide the spending of their funds. It is often a requirement that multiple departments are represented on each committee. Since the school library is typically considered its own department and the school librarian its leader, the possibility of school librarians actively serving on committees is nearly guaranteed. This move keeps school libraries in consideration in important conversations with the school leadership, keeps school librarians' work visible, and gives us regular opportunities to share current data and speak up for the needs of programs.

> *"We need to keep in mind that library numbers and statistics*
> *are pretty meaningless to anyone else unless they are connected*
> *to your school and/or district priorities."*
>
> —Len Bryan

In the article "How to Speak Administrator," two school administrators Andrew Maxey and Mike Daria (2018) address school librarians directly on how to effectively advocate for the school library to their own administration. They advise school librarians that "data is the language of educational leaders." Maxey and Daria go on to write that school librarians can use this "language" to communicate important details such as the state of the collection, its age, and the number of books available. In your school, "Where are the examples of students who are better readers *because they read a lot*?" (Maxey and Daria 2018). Use data to show administrators the connection between self-directed learning and strengthening reading.

"Put Your Money Where Your Mouth Is."

Budgets are moral documents and every day school librarians purchase materials that share values. As school librarians advocate for libraries to be more inclusive and more reflective of the populations served, and advocate for the digital rights and responsibilities of students, we need to commit to making purchases that reflect the same goals. Librarians must relentlessly remind stakeholders of the impact of the library and the work that it takes to lead students into lives of active reading and learning. In order to do this, we must have an accessible diverse collection that functions as a critical piece to students' academic needs, inquiries, and personal interests. As a core piece of what school librarians do, enabling students to exercise their intellectual freedom and their right for full access to information tops the list.

The library collection and program must strive to be current, culturally relevant, and well rounded. Often there is a chasm between the size of a budget that is needed to curate a library collection and the actual amount budgeted for the school librarian's use. Due to this common problem, librarians must treat every purchase like a careful investment in the advancement of the library and as a reflection of the school community for which we serve. School librarians pursue financial support for the program beyond the basic budget in the form of grants or community fund-raisers. This extra effort is proof that we invest our time and expertise in our libraries. We go beyond words to actions that demonstrate our values. We put our actions where our values are.

Committing to Communication and Consistency

Determining the best ways to communicate with each group in your school community is a powerful step in the right advocacy direction. Establishing consistent modes and methods helps get those important and relevant updates to our target audience. When stakeholders start to notice your patterns and faithful action of keeping them "in the loop," your commitment to the growth and inclusion of all parts of the community will be evident. Then, you can add specific resources and programming into the mix to back up this communication.

For example, when establishing a monthly library newsletter, one way to be sure to speak to all intended audiences is to create different sections for different readers as opposed to creating several versions. The main body could be recent happenings and partnerships in the library, which is relevant for all readers. One section could be "Admin Corner" in which the school librarian shares circulation data or number of classes or students and classroom teachers using the library. Another might be "Student Connections" in which the school librarian shares upcoming tutoring opportunities, club invitations, or student-centered events happening with dates, times, and connections such as social media handles.

Establishing Connections

Reaching out and staying connected to one another these days is easier and more convenient than ever. With the creation and adoption of digital connections, and more recently the rise in social media, the school librarian has the ability to become a part of the everyday habits of students, families, teachers and staff, and other essential groups within the school community. As a department that stands on its own, and its programs relevant to all other departments, school libraries can "corner the market" on social media. Sharing information and other types of important content via social media is less time intensive than e-mail and newsletters. With a far and wide reach and with the potential to gain attention from stakeholders visually through relevant student- and learning-centered photos and video content, connections made through social media outlets are a powerful tool for advocacy.

Many times, our success in making connections can be anticipated through careful consideration of the groups we intend to reach. This is where building knowledge around the needs of your school community comes in. An e-mailed or printed newsletter or a library Facebook page might be the best medium for adult stakeholders—colleagues, school administrators, and district leadership. Since teens tend to check their e-mail less and their social media more, posting on Instagram or Twitter may be a more effective way to get library news and information out to students. Since younger children neither have social media nor tend to habitually check their e-mail, school announcements via ASB or the office, wall, and library displays or flyers around school might be a better way to connect with them. Surveying these groups, curating a list of e-mails for a library newsletter, sharing a newsletter, or trying out a combination of different methods are a few of many options you could choose to make strong connections.

Consistency in Contact

A common thread in effectively advocating for the school library to the school administration is a consistent form of communication and continual, specific invitations. A library newsletter is a powerful tool to help keep the school administrators, not to mention the whole school community, abreast of the work of the school librarian and learning taking place in the library.

There is also power in inviting administrators and even district leaders into the library to witness our work firsthand.

> *"Now more than ever your school administrator needs to hear*
> *your voice and know that you are there to support them and*
> *the culture of teaching and learning."*
>
> —*Kathryn Roots Lewis*

Administrators generally love to see effective work in action in their schools. Send them a meeting invite for a specific time or series of times a classroom is coming in for lessons or when events are taking place that result from the work and planning of the school librarian. They will need to hear directly from you to know the "whats, hows, whens and wheres" of these opportunities. They will come if their schedule allows. And especially if they get multiple invitations from you or, better yet, from students and others requesting their presence.

The Courage to Advocate

Advocating for the school library to the local community and beyond is most powerfully done when the focus is on the students—their needs, their experiences, and their work. It takes courage to speak up for what is important for them and for the library program or for what is being largely misunderstood or misrepresented. Parents and community members time and again mistake the libraries of their own youth, the libraries of the past, for today's "future-ready" school library. One of the best and easiest ways to make this connection is to involve students as much as possible in this work. Let students' voices ring through all that is done and all that is emphasized involving the library program. Show stakeholders that the library is needed and is more vibrant than ever while aligning work in the library with the mission and objectives of the school.

Make this work visible by making key connections with administration, staff and parents in leadership roles, school initiatives, and events. Align the work in the library with classroom teachers as much as possible. Ask that the work be highlighted in the library or outside the library walls on display. Ask to be a guest writer in a monthly school-to-home publication or, better yet, be a featured part of each edition. Whatever it is that gets the spotlight on the work being done by the school librarian in the library, both by and for the benefit of students, have the courage to pursue it, repeat it, and make the most of it. Some of the most fruitful advocacy initiatives can come from opportunities we take that involve stepping out of our comfort zones to make new connections—all for the continuation of the support and vitality of the school library.

School librarians have consistently been reluctant to share our work, amplify the voices of our programs, or put the work we are doing first when district budget cuts loom. When school librarians advocate, we are literally fighting to save the reading lives of students and prevent the very real possibility that school libraries may disappear. It is the practice and continued efforts of school librarians to make our work visible that will ensure students have access to rich and diverse collections of texts with varied perspectives, equitable access to technology tools, and an advocate for inclusion in the person of a state-certified school librarian.

If school librarians do not amplify and "brag" about the work that is happening in our libraries, nobody will know the work we are doing or be able to speak to the value we provide. Some librarians may feel that promoting our work is cumbersome and that the benefits of advocacy are difficult to measure. Some think that social media exists only to advertise and brag; that it only shows the best version of something or someone constantly posting the highs and not any of the lows. This might be true. By sharing the whole process from the start through the messy but productive middle to the finished product tells a complete learning story. If we stay optimistic and keep our message positive, we will be proud of all of it.

VIGNETTE: CONTROL THE NARRATIVE, OR ONE WILL BE WRITTEN FOR YOU

TuesD Chambers

District-Level Advocacy

The Seattle Public School (SPS) District is the largest district in the state of Washington. We are a diverse, urban school district with over one hundred schools, with a state-certified librarian serving at least part-time at almost every site. Prior to the 2018 academic year, elementary librarians were reduced to part-time, thereby compromising the reading lives of 55,000 students. In 2018, district administrators attempted to again "solve" the looming budget crisis by reducing secondary librarians to part-time as well. Underserving the literacy learning needs of students and their classroom teachers should be unconscionable, but the mindset of the district, when financial push comes to shove, can only be interpreted as giving this message: school librarians are expendable. The SPS Library Newsletter was born from a need to share the work we do as librarians and combat that erroneous idea.

Many educator colleagues, administrators, and families don't know or understand the integral role librarians play in schools. The SPS Library Newsletter started as a communication tool with messages from the district school library program director, highlights of the work of both elementary and secondary librarians, resources on racial equity, technology tools, and opportunities to advocate for library resources and programs.

Prior to this crisis, librarians needed a way to connect with one another across our geographically vast district. Everyone agreed more communication as a library corps would only improve our work. Librarians also needed a resource to highlight the great work being done and a vehicle to amplify that work to colleagues, site administrators, district personnel, and school board members. From this need and a belief that all educators want to continue to improve their practice, we shared the SPS Library Newsletter far and wide.

Site-Level Advocacy

The SPS Library Newsletter was published monthly with highlights and articles written by librarians across the district. At first, the newsletter was mainly used as a tool to communicate and share with one another but quickly turned into a fantastic tool for advocacy. The principals and directors of each featured librarian received an e-mail about the great work they had been doing. Each highlighted librarian was also showcased in personal correspondence to their school board representative. The SPS Library Newsletter amplified school librarians' work—work that was aligned with the SPS Strategic Plan and goals for literacy within the district.

Like many types of advocacy efforts requiring voluntary participation, adding a little dose of healthy competition to the mix can spice up interest in any activity. This is the case in many library programs as well. Not only does the SPS Library Newsletter highlight the good work of the school librarian, it also draws in groups that might not normally frequent library events or support the library, including students' families, school administrators, community members, and those in important decision-making roles such as district leadership. Directing attention toward a school site hosting literacy-centered events that focus on the reading lives and learning of students is a powerful way to gain the attention and momentum needed to make a point: school librarians matter. We transform teaching and learning. We make a difference for students, classroom teachers, and school communities.

TuesD serves as a teacher-librarian at Ballard High School in Seattle Public Schools. She has been an educator for twenty years and earned her MEd in professional development and leadership with library media. She teaches digital leadership, literacy, and twenty-first-century skills and was chosen as the Washington State Teacher Librarian of the Year for 2019.

Erin Godfrey Bethel

Two years ago, I applied for a grant through a local organization to begin an exciting reading program for students. We received $2,000 from Graduate Tacoma to begin implementing the Global Reading Challenge (GRC). Although this competition had been around in Washington State for many years, Tacoma School District had yet to experience the incredible impact of this program, which involved students in fourth and fifth grade reading nine books that reflect diversity and inclusion, and a range of interests and reading levels. This program was highly successful across the state, but unfortunately did not have a presence in our district.

I had two specific goals in mind for this grant. First, I wanted to promote a love for reading. As I often say when advocating for libraries, "We read for the LOVE of reading, not the level (of reading)." Sadly, and too often, I've heard classroom teachers instructing students to choose a book that was the right level. Adopting this program would ensure students had access to a wide variety of diverse texts available to them purely for the love of reading. Secondly, in addition to advocating for the library and our services, I also wanted to provide a space for kids who might not feel accepted, wanted, or included in other places in our school. For years now, I've been working through promotions on our school website, posts on social media, becoming a teacher-leader within our school community and PTA, and as always, advertise the library as a HUB for all. Our motto is: anyone and everyone are welcome. I wanted to make that tangible.

For several months, I met with students during our lunch recess once weekly. They read diverse literature in teams and competed in a trivia-style competition. Along with Suzanna Panter, program manager for (Tacoma) School Libraries, I got to choose the text for the competition. Our selection process was extremely purposeful and one of the important outcomes of this project.

We've been able to spread the word and theme for students to develop a love of reading. Students worked with their team members through research, discussions, and questioning. Our first year we had twenty-three participants; this year we had thirty-seven participants at our school alone. In the second year, four schools participated. The growth was apparent as our numbers extended beyond our Washington Elementary teams to hundreds of students at other elementary schools.

Not only did our teams experience the thrill of the competition, but each school held their own challenge as an assembly. This was the best advertising ever for recruiting GRC members. Our district competition was also a huge event with families, parents, and peers attending. Thinking strategically, I invited both Tacoma's Superintendent Carla Santorno and Deputy Superintendent Josh Garcia who came to watch our competition.

In order to continue growing and expanding the GRC program, we needed to be seen and highlighted throughout the district. The first year of our competition my advocacy included sharing images on Instagram and Twitter and informing our school staff of the great benefits of the program. This past year, I reached out to my fellow librarians and to community partners. I was able to obtain donations from businesses to help with the cost of team shirts for our students and for the competition supplies.

The initial grant funds were used for purchasing books for participating schools. Not only would we get the opportunity to advertise this program through months of meetings, announcements, and the competition itself, but the books would be forever found in the libraries for students to read. Through our promotions, we gained momentum for our third year of the competition. Parents sent e-mails and notes expressing how much of an impact this program was making and would continue to make on their children. Comments ranged from "I also wanted to say how great the diversity of books was," to the program is "a platform for some really thoughtful discussions." And "I will always remember the conversation we had about that book," to "We greatly appreciate you taking on this extra commitment and hope you see what a difference it is making in the lives of your students." Each year, our GRC competition will continue to grow and make a difference in many young readers' lives.

Prior to the COVID-19 pandemic in spring of 2020, the winning team was scheduled to appear on TV Tacoma, an award-winning government-access television station. Now, in our seventh month of social distancing and mask wearing, promotion and implementation will need to look very different. When virtual learning is all but inevitable for the foreseeable future, I'll be approaching our programming in creative ways. My hope is that more students will participate even if it's from a physical distance and in front of a screen. Although we librarians and educators work to offer all of our students access to the technology and tools they need to be successful, the specific messaging of our library and the GRC mantra doesn't waiver or change. It isn't for the level of reading; it's for the *love* of reading. And there's no doubt that in GRC, we share a lot of love.

Erin is a teacher-librarian at Washington Elementary in Tacoma, Washington. She has over fifteen years of experience teaching, received her national board certification in 2008, and renewed it in 2018. She has an MEd, has presented for the Washington Library Association, is a Microsoft innovative educator, and is an adjunct professor at Antioch University. Connect at @mrsbethelsbookshelf.

Public Relations Efforts Build Advocates

Advocacy is essential for school librarians for many reasons. Simply stated, "People don't know what they don't know." True advocacy strives to make good work visible and makes this information accessible to those who don't know about the learning and connections happening in the school library. It also asks stakeholders to speak up for the library program. When our underlying message is "Libraries are essential because they are good for kids. Here's why and how . . ." we need to act on that by creating multiple ways to share this message by amplifying multiple voices and offering stakeholders varied levels of involvement in our programs.

Advocacy is a necessary component in effectively getting the point across that the school library led by a state-certified school librarian is a nonnegotiable asset to every school. The best and most effective way for school librarians to get this message across is when students, classroom teachers, and community members are the voices and faces of the school library. We can share their voices and faces in photos, videos, newsletters, social media, or a combination of some or all of those things. It takes a special kind of curator to gather these voices for others to see and hear until our advocates' voices become impossible to ignore. It takes a certified school librarian leader who is a library and librarian advocate.

Reflection Questions

1. What is one method or example of advocacy described in this chapter that you are now inspired to get to work on? Why?

2. Whether you have come from a noneducation background, the classroom, or are serving in a school library, what ideas in this chapter ring true for you?

3. What types of advocacy have you led or been a part of in your career or schooling experience that had you nodding your head in agreement as you read this chapter? What were the outcomes?

References

Maxey, Andrew, and Mike Daria. 2018 "How to Speak Administrator." *School Library Journal*, October 3. Available at https://www.slj.com?detailStory =1810-Speaking-Administrator. Accessed October 1, 2020.

Ray, Mark. 2012. "Big Picture Advocacy: Making Fifteen Minutes Count." *School Library Monthly* 28(6): 29–31.

Sierra, Kristin Fraga. 2018. "Creating a Culture of Reading: Revisiting Skype." *School Library Journal*, August 21. Available at https://www.slj.com?detail Story=creating-culture-reading-revisiting-skype. Accessed October 1, 2020.

Vercelletto, Christina. 2016. "Future Ready Schools Announces Project to Recognize School Librarians as Leaders in Learning Transformation." *School Library Journal*, June 30. Available at https://www.slj.com?detailStory=future -ready-schools-announces-project-to-recognize-school-librarians-as-leaders -in-school-transformation. Accessed October 1, 2020.

PART III

A Collaborative Culture
of Learning

CHAPTER 9

Collaboration

Judi Moreillon

Collaboration is THE key to co-creating a values-centered
culture of deeper learning.

Dynamic School Cultures

I believe collaboration is the key to influencing the values and changing
the priorities of members of every school learning community. Creating a
school culture is about connecting values, ideas, and information through
relationships among stakeholders. Culture is a way of life composed "of
shared beliefs, knowledge, attitudes, language, behaviors, social interactions,
and more. Cultures are created by people over time. Cultures are dynamic;
they are not fixed. Cultures change as people's needs and norms change"
(Moreillon 2018b, 170). School librarians can play a pivotal role in initiating,
maintaining, and sustaining transformation in our schools.

When members of a learning community agree to transform their culture,
they must revisit and refresh their school's mission and vision. In the process, they will reassess and realign their values. As they move forward, the
community will then set about changing their priorities in order to reach
their goals. All along the way, stakeholders will collaborate with one another,
revise, and enact agreements to ensure that all members receive the benefits
of this transformative process. The collaborative conversations and actions
taken create the community's transformed culture.

"In a functioning democracy, we must slowly build consensus among
diverse individuals around core values in order to transform culture" (Lee and
Eisen-Markowitz 2018, 95). School librarians can be essential leaders in
transforming school culture because we work alongside administrators and

every educator colleague and are charged with serving every student and their families. We can capitalize on our position as educators who colead from the largest classroom in the school—the library. By focusing on and accelerating our collaborative work, school librarians can be leaders in changing values and priorities and moving forward with our colleagues toward school transformation that meets the needs of all students and families.

Collaborating school librarians can also make connections that result in deeper learning. We know the taught curriculum across the grade levels. The literacies, thinking skills, and dispositions students practice through an integrated school library program are transferrable to every discipline and to lifelong learning. If we have done our homework, we have influenced teaching and learning practices throughout the building through coordination, cooperation, collaboration, coteaching, and just-in-time professional development. With these connections and the most diverse and greatest number of resources in multiple formats and reading levels, school librarians can secure our seat at the leadership table.

Mission and Goals

"Leaders maintain an understanding of what the mission and goals of an organization are and how these can be fulfilled" (Riggs 2001). Today's education leaders seek to move their colleagues or organizations forward to embrace and enact education equity, develop responsive and effective instructional strategies, and utilize the diverse resources and digital tools of our times. School librarians are positioned to serve as literacy leaders. As a district superintendent recently noted: "Often times I hear people say librarians support literacy work in classrooms. We need to change the word 'support' to 'lead'" (Doherty 2018).

When a school or district is revisiting their mission and setting new priorities, school librarians, with our global view of our learning communities, have an invaluable perspective. Our contact with all classroom educators and students helps us "read" the school. We know which students are accessing the resources of the library for academic and personal purposes and which are effectively applying digital tools to meet learning outcomes. We know whether or not classroom teachers are promoting independent reading and choice. We know which educators are facilitating student-led inquiry learning and creating opportunities for relevant, differentiated, personalized, equitable access to deeper learning. From the heart of the school—the library—we have our fingers on the pulse of the taught curriculum in our schools.

When it is time to reconsider our school's mission and goals, school librarians know which policies, procedures, and practices are working for all students, educators, and families. Alongside our site administrators and other teacher-leaders, we can colead the change process. By enacting librarian values through the library program, school librarians model the change we want to see. We build trust when we follow through with our commitments to equity, diversity, inclusion, and intellectual freedom. When we are grounded in our values, we can demonstrate courage in the face of adversity.

Change Creates Leadership Opportunities

"If leadership is (a) social influence process of enlisting the aid and support of others in the accomplishment of a common task, a leader is consequently someone whom you would follow where you would not normally go alone, someone who rallies people to a better future" (Haycock 2017, 2). One primary activity of leaders is to inspire and influence the thinking and behaviors of others. When school librarians embrace a leadership role, we have the opportunity to cocreate an equitable, inclusive school culture that truly transforms education. It is a way to enact social justice in our communities.

"The three most important words in education are: relationships, relationships, relationships. Without them, we have nothing."

—*George Couros*

Collaboration is an indispensable behavior of school librarian leaders who help all library stakeholders reach their capacity. In order to achieve a high-impact level of service, school librarian leaders nurture, develop, and sustain relationships with all library stakeholders. We build confidence by continuously improving our skill sets, including culturally responsive teaching and technological innovations. School librarians develop our communication skills in order to listen and respond to the ever-evolving needs of learners—students and educators alike. Through relationships and communication, school librarians lead with confidence (Everhart and Johnston 2016). Through leadership and collaboration, school librarians cocreate and colead educational change.

Instructional Partnerships: Creating Advocates

When asked whom they serve, "most [school librarians] would answer students, yet the primary clientele in terms of power, impact, and effect would be teachers" (Haycock 2017, 3). Classroom-library collaboration for instruction is one central strategy that helps school librarians position their work and the library program as the hub of academic and personal learning in the school. As instructional partners, school librarians codesign effective instruction, provide and engage in professional learning opportunities with colleagues, and improve our own teaching practice in the process. By doing so, we engender advocates for the library program. Collaboration with colleagues is a necessity, not an option.

"Collaborate" is one of the American Association of School Librarians (2018) shared foundations and a competency for students. Therefore, school librarians are called on to take the necessary risks to model, practice, and achieve their own level of competence in collaborative work. Collaborating educators believe that their instructional practices develop at a much greater rate with more assured improvements when they collaborate. As centralized instructional partners, school librarians help classroom teachers reach student learning outcome targets based in the classroom curriculum and work to solve instructional challenges with their colleagues (see Berg, Kramer, and Werle 2019).

VIGNETTE: MEANINGFUL COLLABORATION

Matt King

Five years ago, I transitioned from a first-grade classroom to our school library. When reviewing Missouri library standards and how I was going to be evaluated, collaboration was a focus area. During district library meetings, collaboration was discussed. Often librarians spoke of the importance of collaboration but lacked system-wide supports for such endeavors. In fact, many librarians believed that providing books to classroom teachers on a specific topic was enough and labeled it collaboration. I questioned that. In fact, being a new librarian, I did not understand how providing books on frogs for a second-grade lesson was collaboration. Isn't collaboration more than just providing resources on a specific topic?

Two years ago, I switched school districts and began my education specialist's degree. I wanted to focus my thesis on collaboration because research tells us how impactful collaboration can be. Throughout the course of my research, I found foundational theories about levels of collaboration. These theories were used to guide my view of meaningful collaboration. Montiel-Overall (2005) indicated four levels of collaboration consisting of coordination, cooperation, integrated instruction, and finally integrated curriculum. I believe that meaningful collaboration happens at the higher levels. Meaningful collaboration is when classroom standards and library standards are integrated completely. These standards are taught and evaluated collectively.

Theory into Practice

In order to understand meaningful collaboration, I instituted a collaborative process in my school. Classroom teachers and I developed

Grade Level:	Topic: Ecosystems
_____ Kindergarten	Subject(s): Science and Writing

Grade Level:
_____ Kindergarten
_____ 1st Grade
_____ 2nd Grade
_____ 3rd Grade
__X__ 4th Grade
_____ 5th Grade

Week: September 16

Lesson:

Classroom:
- Lessons about ecosystems
- Lessons about informative writing

Library:
- Lesson about conducting research
  - Using Explora
  - Citing Sources

Topic: Ecosystems

Subject(s): Science and Writing

Classroom Standards from Missouri Learning Standards

4.LS1.A.1: Construct an argument that plants and animals have internal and external structures that function to support survival, growth, behavior, and plant reproduction.

ELA B1: Write informative/explanatory texts that: a) introduce a topic using a topic sentence in an introductory paragraph b) develop the topic into supporting paragraphs from sources, using topic sentences with facts, details, examples, and quotations c) use specific, relevant, and accurate words that are suited to the topic, audience, and purpose d) contain information using students' original language except when using direct quotations from a source e) use transitions to connect categories of information f) use text structures when useful g) create a conclusion paragraph related to the information

Library Standards from Missouri Library Standards

Standard 3: Provides access to information for students, teachers, staff, and administrators to satisfy all learning needs. Teaches information literacy skills to build proficiency for student-driven research and individual creation of knowledge through critical thinking. Promotes equitable access to resources in a variety of formats and services for a variety of needs.
- Quality Indicator 1: Access to information
- Quality Indicator 2: Information literacy skills

Objectives:
- Students will be able to write a four-paragraph essay
- Students will be able to conduct research
- Students will learn about ponds, forests, and prairies

Assessment
- Scoring Guide

Materials
- Nature Unleashed
- Library Website

Adapted from J. Moreillon, *Coteaching Reading Comprehension Strategies in Elementary School Libraries: Maximizing Your Impact* (Chicago: American Library Association, 2013). Licensed under the Creative Commons Attribution-Noncommercial-Share Alike 2.5 License: http://creative commons.org/licenses/by-nc-sa/2.5/.

Figure 9.1 Discovery Elementary School Library collaboration plan.

lessons that incorporated both library and classroom standards using a written collaboration plan. Before this plan, classroom teachers were unaware of library standards. This collaborative process helped educate classroom teachers on the importance of having a highly trained librarian as an instructional partner. We developed a scoring guide to evaluate student learning that combined both standards. We determined who would be responsible for teaching which objectives. Some lessons were taught by me, others were taught by the classroom teacher, and some were cotaught. In the end, we assessed and evaluated student outcomes together. This ecosystems collaboration plan is taken from my thesis (King 2019, 88).

Lessons Learned

From our collaborative efforts, I have learned valuable lessons about what can make meaningful collaboration happen. Many times, teachers are unaware of what skills and resources a librarian can provide. It is imperative for school librarians to promote and advocate for these skills to ensure that their expertise is used throughout the building. When classroom teachers understand what resources a school librarian can offer, collaboration will happen.

Meaningful collaboration is deliberate; it is a predetermined plan. It is not spontaneous. In schools today, common planning times seldom occur between school librarians and classroom teachers. Teachers and librarians have so much on their plates—and finding time to collaborate seems impossible—but the effort is so worthwhile. By meeting outside of school hours, using digital communication and impromptu conversations, a collaborative plan can be developed. These collaborative plans are imperative to ensure deeper levels of collaboration.

Finally, relationships are critical for meaningful collaboration. Classroom teachers and librarians must value the expertise of each other. Taking the time to connect with stakeholders and provide resources allowed teachers in my building to see me as an equal partner with unique areas of expertise, which increased their trust and willingness to collaborate. As a result of our collaborative planning and teaching, all library stakeholders have benefited—students, classroom teachers, administrators, and me, too!

Matt is the school librarian at the Discovery Elementary School, Orchard Farm School District, in St. Charles, Missouri. Matt received the 2019 Greater St. Louis Library Program of the Year Award. He served as the 2020 AASL chapter delegate and was a 2019 ALA emerging leader.

Making the commitment to meaningful classroom-library collaboration is no small act. It means we will not always have "things" our way as we strive to enact our values and spread those values through collaborative work. We will need to negotiate as we align our library program goals and objectives with those of our classroom teacher colleagues. We will bump up against the status quo. We will be called on to meet others where they are as we move alongside them to a better future for our students. In this process, we will invest time and energy in educating others and provide the necessary evidence of benefits and outcomes that support the changes we seek.

Making a Commitment to Core Values in Practice

In each chapter in this book, we, the contributors, have shared our first-hand experiences as well as other school librarians' stories. We have shared our passion for the four core values—equity, diversity, inclusion, and intellectual freedom. As evidenced by our applications in practice, we know passion is not enough. School librarians must collaborate with members of the learning community in order to reach our capacity to enact the core values of our profession. We must develop pathways to enact these values in the field—through relationships, principal-librarian partnerships, leadership, and advocacy.

Shining a light on these bright spots has given us a great deal to consider as we self-assess our own practice and develop strategies for improving our work. If equity only resides in the heart of the school librarian and in the services of the school library, we will not transform teaching and learning for every student every day. All students, classroom educators, and families must have equitable access to the library's resources and the work of school librarians. The very meaning of equity charges us to diffuse values, beliefs, and opportunities throughout the school community.

At this time in history, both nationally and globally, educators must be laser focused on ensuring equitable access to high-quality learning. The opportunity gap created by the unequal distribution of digital tools and broadband during the pandemic has exposed inequities far too familiar to educators. But access to individual or shared technology devices and high-speed Internet are far from the only inequities that undermine student learning in 2020. Other socioeconomic and family-specific factors that support or hinder a student's ability to succeed include food security, health care access, adults' work schedules or how losing one or more jobs affects a family, and older siblings' or adults' ability to support learning. These and school-specific factors were heightened when schooling went 100 percent online in the spring of 2020.

"When you see something that is not right, not fair, not just, you have to speak up. You have to say something; you have to do something."

—*Representative John Lewis*

As this book goes to press, our nation is engaged in a focused conversation about systemic racism. When living through our values, school librarians can serve as catalysts for deep conversations and structural change. Through words, actions, and advocacy, we can guide our schools and districts toward racial justice. When we speak our truth while remaining grounded in our values, we will practice humility and compassion for the challenges faced by decision makers in our schools. At the same time, we will insist on integrity, empathy, and change that move us forward toward a more just education for all students.

School librarians can plant seeds for transformative social justice. We, who hold dear the values of equity, diversity, inclusion, and intellectual freedom, cannot be silent. We are compelled to advocate and act for equitable access to learning opportunities in our schools, districts, and communities. We can purchase and curate diverse resources, but if those resources are used solely in the library, we are not transforming our learning communities. If the school library is the only space in the school where inclusion is a priority, then we have fallen short of our potential to lead change.

If the school librarian is the only educator in the building who embraces and advocates for intellectual freedom, then there will likely be spaces in students' school days where they do not have a voice. The same will be true for educators and families. When school librarians fully educate our administrators and colleagues about the essential practice of free speech, we can help ensure that everyone in the learning community will be given a voice. We can insist that everyone's ideas and opinions are heard and respected. And we can advocate for decision making that takes all voices into account.

Using Our Values as a Foundation for Courage

The ways school librarians address academic, societal, and political inequities cannot be a neutral stance. The daily decisions we make reflect our shared librarianship values, the values of our communities, and our own personal values as well. School librarians who adhere to our value of "access" seek to be fair rather than equal. A neutral library would simply exist and serve those who come through our library doors. On the other hand, when librarians assess the needs of our community and determine how to best help all stakeholders achieve their potential, we will, of necessity, do more for some than for others.

The courage to hold to our values will invariably take school librarians out of our comfort zones. We will be required to stand up for what's fair and equitable rather than what is equal and not necessarily fair. "Our English language learners and their classroom teachers may need more literacy support than our gifted and talented students and their classroom teachers. Youth living in poverty may need access to literacy and technology resources more than our affluent students who have access in their homes or back pockets. Inviting an author from an underrepresented group to provide a literacy event may speak in more personally meaningful and impactful ways to some of our students and families than to others" (Moreillon 2018a).

"The decision to never veer from your cause, to hold yourself accountable to HOW you do things; that's the hardest part."

—*Simon Sinek*

Accountability to Students

Courageous norm breaking may be part of school librarians' contribution to school transformation. Beginning with students, "librarians have unique opportunities to promote choice and voice through a student-centered approach to facility design, instruction, programming, and collection development" (Harper and Deskins 2020, 49). We may ask ourselves questions such as these:

1. How do our facilities meet the needs of students who come to the library to read, study, socialize, and organize?
2. How does our instruction and library programming meet the needs of students from all racial and socioeconomic backgrounds, all gender identities, English language learners, and students with special needs?
3. How do we intentionally involve students in decision making regarding library policies, procedures, and programming as well as in collection development?

Agency is a key component of inquiry learning and reader choice applied to curriculum-based and independent reading. We may have to support students as they grow from compliance-dependent pupils to empowered learners who think critically about ideas and information. When developing students as agents in their own learning process, we will have to disrupt the student-to-educator power differential. We will need to be vocal advocates for our students' intellectual freedom.

School libraries can also be safe spaces for student organizing, another example of youth agency. In any school-based changed movement, educators should follow students' demand: "Ask us—We're the ones in the classroom" (Rojas and Wornum 2018, 27). When students are supported as they use their voices to create change in their lived experience of schooling, they can develop as activists in creating both their present and their future. When young people are at the forefront and center of transforming schools, adults must encourage their leadership.

Not all of our colleagues will be in agreement with these approaches to learning and teaching. Beginning with even one or two like-minded colleagues, we will be able to collect data affirming that student choice and voice is an equity issue as well as a way to improve motivation and academic achievement. Providing students with equitable access to relevant, engaging, and culturally responsive curriculum, resources, and programming must be essential to our mission. We cannot be quiet; we must stand up and advocate for our students.

Accountability to Colleagues

In our collaborative work with classroom teachers and specialists, we will need to be able to hear the words "no thank you" and not give up. Some of our colleagues, for various reasons, will not initially embrace the diversity in resources and programming or a focus on inclusion and intellectual freedom that are central to exemplary library practice. Some will not be on the same page as we are with regard to seeing us as codesigners of instruction who address those priorities. Some will not welcome our work as coteachers who jointly implement lessons and units of instruction. Others may not recognize us as peer educators who share responsibility for assessing student learning outcomes. We may ask ourselves questions such as these:

1. How do our levels of service interface with colleagues on a continuum from cooperation and coordination to collaboration?
2. How are our core values in school librarianship evidenced in our collaborative work with classroom teachers and specialists?
3. How do we succeed in coleading a change process in which our colleagues' voices are heard, respected, and considered?

We will collaborate with colleagues who are enthusiastic and willing collaborators. We will also strive to work with reluctant instructional partners. To all members of the learning community, we will need to demonstrate the benefits of classroom-library collaboration for students as well as for educators' professional learning. This is especially true when sharing our classroom-library collaborative work with administrators.

Accountability to Administrators

As we infuse our practice with our core values, we can grow in our leadership capacity in collaboration with our principals and site-level leaders. For the most part, school principals determine the availability of leadership opportunities for all teacher leaders, including school librarians. Principals' willingness to delegate leadership tasks, support full staffing and library budgets, and promote collaboration and (flexible) scheduling can create openings (or barriers) to school librarian leadership (Johnston 2015). When considering how to effectively collaborate with our principals, we may ask ourselves questions such as these:

1. How do we support our principals' goals and objectives for our learning community?
2. How do we earn trust and demonstrate reliability in our interactions with our principals?
3. How does our collaborative work with our principals and other decision makers positively impact learning and teaching throughout our school and district?

If our principals or district-level leaders go out on a limb to support our efforts toward change through library programs, they will need to know we can and will deliver on our promises. We will need to ensure that our work helps others meet their needs to increase student learning outcomes and helps all members of the learning community reach their capacity. We must practice integrity and follow-through in our professional work.

Leadership and Innovation

"Whatever the innovation, building and sustaining a culture of collaboration provides the necessary foundation for change" (Moreillon 2018b, 152). Principals are charged with leading the school in developing a vision, setting and achieving goals, and creating the conditions in which students, educators, and families reach their capacity. A collaborative culture is one condition that supports individuals, groups, and whole schools in reaching their potential. In a collaborative school culture, principals "endorse a whole school, 21st-century learning environment where educators model collaboration for students as they collaborate; encourage a culture of innovation, risk taking, and high expectations; and acknowledge the actions school librarians take to shape a school culture of deep learning" (Todd, Gordon, and Lu 2012, xxii).

Principals who empower educators, including librarians, to lead alongside them further the collaborative culture in their schools. Principals and school librarians can colead in a collaborative school culture. If library programs are to reach capacity, school librarians must invest in building mutually beneficial partnerships with principals. Together, school librarians and principals colead a change process that spreads innovation throughout their schools.

Effective school librarians and principals extend their impact beyond the school walls to work with families and other community members. A close working relationship between principals and school librarians helps us share our insights into the various components of the learning community and how to improve outcomes for all. Working as a team to reach out to families and district-level decision makers is a winning strategy for both principals and librarians. When we make our leadership visible to others and invite their feedback and input, we increase the likelihood of success in building a culture of learning.

Cocreating a Culture of Deeper Learning

Leadership in schools, at all instructional levels, has been described "as an essential condition of innovation and change" (Mardis 2013, 41). In order to transform our schools to meet the needs of today's students and address the societal changes in our communities and country, we must engage in respectful, productive conversations. We must work together to identify fresh ideas and strategies for improving teaching and learning. We must take risks, experiment, self-assess, and adjust our practice with the support and encouragement of our colleagues.

If innovation is a process of thinking that involves creating something new and better (George Couros paraphrase), then school librarians, as collaborators and professional developers, will always be seeking improvement. As Senge and his colleagues suggest: schools that learn are "places where everyone, young and old, would continuously develop and grow in each other's company; they would be incubation sites for continuous change and growth. If we want the world to improve, in other words, then we need schools that learn" (Senge et al. 2012, 4–5).

There are no shortcuts to creating, nurturing and sustaining schools that learn. There are no short cuts to culture building. Educators must develop trust and invest in our own and our colleagues' continuous learning. Serving as coleaders and collaborators in schools that learn, school librarians can be the keys that unlock the potential of our school cultures to grow, to change, and to transform.

The core values of school librarianship require that school librarians become activists who spread core librarian values through classroom-library collaboration. It is only when school curricula are examined, reexamined, and transformed through a lens of equity, diversity, inclusion, and intellectual freedom that school librarians will have reached our capacity as change makers in our schools. When school librarians serve as instructional partners to coplan and coimplement learning opportunities and coassess student learning outcomes, we organically and authentically create opportunities to share, enact, and spread our core values. We can be catalysts for values-based culture building.

My middle school English language arts (ELA) classroom is lovingly named the Literacy Lounge. The climate is soothing and welcoming; we enjoy flexible seating and work areas throughout the space, and books are plentiful, of course. The culture is built on literacy as an important part of becoming reflective learners and lifelong readers. The students and I frequently refer to our driving question, "How can we share our love of literacy with our school and community?" We engage in project-based learning (PBL), Passion Projects/Genius Hour, and make innovative learning a priority. And what better way to enhance our learning experiences than to team up with our Horizon Middle School (HMS) librarian!

The Literacy Lounge Meets the Discovery Den

For some classroom teachers, it is necessary to grow a mind-set that understands how a library and librarian can benefit our students and our own teaching. However, it seems there are some barriers to overcome in this area. My librarian Kat has faced those challenges. I interviewed Kat for this vignette. Here are some excerpts.

Jenni: What feedback have you been given on barriers to collaboration in the library or with a librarian?

Kat: "If you build it, they will come." As our principal Dr. Tabby Rabenberg once told me, "building relationships with teachers (as with students) begins with one simple step: taking each person where they are at." There are those natural coteachers, like you, Jenni! Then, there are those who would love the opportunity but just don't know where to begin. Our district-level library director Misti Werle developed a survey that asked teachers to identify barriers to collaboration. Horizon teachers currently view the following as barriers: needing two librarians (1,200 students, grades 6–8); knowing what I'm willing and able to coteach; and easy access to online resources with how-to tutorials and ideas for integrating technology tools into their curriculum.

Jenni: When I share with colleagues the collaborative projects we coteach, they seem to become more inquisitive about the library and what it has to offer. I think sharing my positive experiences has helped other teachers reach out to you. How do you encourage and provide positive partnerships?

Kat: The foundation of our library, the Horizon Discovery Den, is solid. Our mission and vision statements encompass the North Dakota Library and Technology Content Standards, AASL Library Standards, PBL competencies, and the 4Cs (Critical Thinking, Creativity, Communication, Collaboration) +1 (Content). The Den's inviting and innovative PAWS (learning spaces that students can reserve online) and tools empower students to personalize learning as they "Discover their PAWSibilities!" To break down teachers' perceived barriers and build relationships, I have designed interactive tools, such as a "Presentation Tools, Tutorials and Templates" slideshow and offer workshops for credit to encourage teachers to include us in the learning process with students.

Effective Instructional Partnerships and Deeper Learning

True instructional partnerships help provide a deeper learning opportunity for students. ELA teachers have a distinct advantage as our ELA standards meld effortlessly with the librarian standards, especially when we are working on research skills and inquiry. Coteaching these lessons has added an aspect of relief by sharing the workload and a bit of fun during the process.

Jenni: When my teaching team plans PBL or I challenge my students with Passion Projects/Genius Hour, I always come to you for coplanning ideas and support during the whole process. How has that helped you understand the classroom structure and teaching strategies, promote voice and choice, engage students, and assess them in their learning?

Kat: I still remember the first time you walked into the Den to collaborate with me. I was fired up by your "let's get down to business" attitude. You spelled out expected student outcomes tied to specific standards and shared some of your previous projects. I was awestruck by your organization and creativity! Then, you asked me what we could do together to make this an engaging and successful learning experience for all students. After catching my breath and asking a few clarifying questions, it was "off to the races"! That was the start of a true instructional partnership.

Jenni: We all have our areas of expertise, but I am of the belief that teachers need to go beyond the walls of their classroom and reach out to their librarian to support the learning outcomes of our students. Librarians have a depth of knowledge that teachers may be unaware of, and the library can be an extension of the classroom. How has the collaborative process changed your vision of what a librarian/library can become?

Kat: Just like Bartholomew Cubbins, librarians wear many hats! My everyday "hat" is to provide the highest level of service and partnership based on student learning outcomes. When collaborating with teachers on project design, implementation, assessment, and reflection, I am faithfully steered by the "Levels of Library Services and Instructional

Partnerships" codeveloped by our district library director Misti Werle and Judi Moreillon (Moreillon 2018b, 28). Our library program continues to evolve because of amazing opportunities to train with educational leaders like coteaching consultant Anne Beninghof and coaching guide Steve Barkley.

Jenni: Teachers are challenged with planning for distance learning due to the COVID-19 pandemic. I think it is imperative to stay connected with kids, continue to promote reading and provide access to the library, however that may look. How can librarians support teachers and students during this time?

Kat: "Ask and you shall receive." The day before our district switched to distance learning, our principal stopped by the classroom where I was coteaching. She asked me to touch base with teachers who might need help with online resources like Google Classroom and Meet. The following week, I e-mailed all teachers and based on their numerous replies, I created the following online tools:

- HMS Online Oasis, a choice board of digital books, read-alouds, and other resources offered for free during distance learning.
- HMS Online PAWSibilities ("evolved" version of the slideshow mentioned previously).
- Collections by Destiny, over 275 sets of how-to tutorials, nonfiction and fiction books in all formats, and teams for educators to curate their own collections.
- And I also stayed connected with students, colleagues, and administrators alike via laptop phone, e-mails, virtual meetings, and curbside checkout.

Jenni: Students are comfortable with you because you reinvented the Discovery Den as a student-centered space by creating the PAWS and sharing the possibilities for learning experiences with staff. My "aha moment" took place during one of our cotaught projects when a student was waiting in a line to ask me a question. He got tired of waiting and said, "Never mind. I know Ms. Berg will know what to do." This solidified my belief that students will see the librarian as their "teacher" if you involve the librarian in the whole learning experience.

As library director Misti Werle states, "The school library is a natural vehicle to drive transformation when improving PBL teaching practices and implementing inquiry learning" (Berg, Kramer, and Werle 2019, 34). My advice to teachers and librarians alike: take the first step and just *ask* about a collaborative opportunity. Don't be afraid to start the conversation or invite colleagues to partner in learning. Take the risk. The PAWSibilities are endless between a classroom teacher and their school librarian!

> Jenni, twenty-three-year educator, holds a master's of education degree and a bachelor's in elementary education from the University of North Dakota, and is licensed in middle school English/reading and elementary grades K–8. She currently teaches English language arts at Horizon Middle School in Bismarck, North Dakota, where she regularly collaborates with her school librarian Kat Berg.
>
> Kat has twenty-six years of teaching/library experience in grades 5–12. She holds a master's degree in library science from St. Cloud State University and a bachelor of arts degree in elementary education, secondary education, English, and Spanish. She is currently the librarian serving in the Horizon Middle School Library, also known as the Discovery Den.

"Adult learning (and leading) in schools is best implemented at the point of practice" (Moreillon and Ballard 2013, vi). When we coplan, coteach, and coassess student learning, classroom teachers and school librarians provide reciprocal mentorship for one another. Classroom-library coteaching creates a context for job-embedded professional development that is intended to provide educators with instructional and cultural interventions that "help create new norms that foster experimentation, collaboration, and continuous improvement" (Guskey 2000, x). When new norms are developed and practiced, school culture can change. Through instructional partnerships with colleagues, school librarians can colead that change.

Inventing the Future—Together

Whether you are a preservice, newly practicing, or seasoned school librarian, we hope our book has helped you find support for embracing a leadership role in your school. Whether you are responding to school culture crises, meeting administrative or faculty changes, responding to book challenges, and other points in practice that test our shared school librarian values, commitment, and courage, we hope you have found support for meeting these situations head on with confidence. We hope you will join us in the chorus and demonstrate, in your daily practice, the critical importance of school librarians' unique contributions to our school learning communities and by extension to literacy learning at large.

> *"The best way to predict the future is to invent it."*
>
> —*Alan Kay*

As literacy leaders, school librarians must take action to cocreate a more just and equitable educational experience for and with youth. It is, therefore, imperative for us to engage in reflection and continuously improve our practice. Through collaboration with others, we can coinvent a future to meet the deeper learning needs for all students, the instructional needs of our colleagues, and the achievement needs of our administrators. School librarians advocate for deeper learning; we can be leaders in a culture of learning.

We, the contributors, hope we have given you moments of inspiration, prompted your deep thinking and reflection, and shared with you experiences as guides that can help you lead in your learning community. We hope you have gained a few more strategies to serve as role models for school librarian values: equity, diversity, inclusion, and intellectual freedom. We hope you will use your voice to affirm your commitment to library values and have the courage to enact them in collaboration with library stakeholders. We remain in the chorus beside you, school librarian leaders, as you stand up today and tomorrow for the hard things.

Reflection Questions

1. With whom in your school do you share your vision for building a collaborative culture of learning?
2. What is your definition of deeper learning, and how do you promote deeper learning through classroom-library collaboration?
3. In order to achieve a school culture of deeper learning, what role have you played or will you play in bringing conversations and actions related to social justice to the fore in your teaching, school, district, and community?

References

American Association of School Librarians. 2018. *National School Library Standards for Learners, School Librarians, and School Libraries*. Chicago: American Library Association.

Berg, Kat, Jenni Kramer, and Misti Werle. 2019. "Implementing & Evaluating Instructional Partnerships." *Knowledge Quest* 47(3): 32–38.

Doherty, Sean. 2018. *School Library Journal* Leadership Summit. Brooklyn, New York.

Everhart, Nancy, and Melissa P. Johnston. 2016. "A Proposed Theory of School Librarian Leadership: A Meta-Ethnographic Approach." *School Library Research* 19. Available at http://www.ala.org/aasl/sites/ala.org.aasl/files/content/aaslpubsandjournals/slr/vol19/SLR_ProposedTheory_V19.pdf. Accessed October 1, 2020.

Guskey, Thomas. 2000. *Evaluating Professional Development*. Thousand Oaks, CA: Corwin Press.

Harper, Meghan, and Liz Deskins. 2020. "Fostering and Sustaining Student Voice in the Library." *School Library Connection* (May–June): 49.

Haycock, Ken. 2017. "Leadership from the Middle: Building Influence for Change." In *The Many Faces of School Library Leadership,* 2nd ed., ed. S. Coatney and V. H. Harada, 1–12. Santa Barbara, CA: Libraries Unlimited.

Johnston, Melissa. 2015. "Distributed Leadership Theory for Investigating Teacher Librarian Leadership." *School Libraries Worldwide* 21: 39–57.

King, Matthew. 2019. "The Examination of Meaningful Collaboration between Classroom Teachers and a School Librarian in an Elementary School." Education Specialist thesis, University of Central Missouri.

Lee, Sally, and Elana "E. M." Eisen-Markowitz. 2018. "Teachers Unite! Organizing School Communities for Transformative Justice." In *Lift Us Up, Don't Push Us Out: Voices from the Front Lines of the Educational Justice Movement,* ed. Mark R. Warren, 92–100. Boston: Beacon Press.

Mardis, Marcia. 2013. "Transfer, Lead, Look Forward: Further Study of Preservice School Librarians' Development." *Journal of Education for Library and Information Science* 54(1): 37–54.

Montiel-Overall, Patricia. 2005. "Toward a Theory of Collaboration for Teachers and Librarians." *School Library Media Research* 8: 1–31. Available at http://www.ala.org/aasl/sites/ala.org.aasl/files/content/aaslpubsandjournals/slr/vol8/SLMR_TheoryofCollaboration_V8.pdf. Accessed October 1, 2020.

Moreillon, Judi. 2018a. "Libraries and Neutrality." *School Librarian Leadership* blog (June 4). Available at https://tinyurl.com/sllblog060418. Accessed October 1, 2020.

Moreillon, Judi. 2018b. *Maximizing School Librarian Leadership: Building Connections for Learning and Advocacy.* Chicago: American Library Association.

Moreillon, Judi, and Susan D. Ballard, eds. 2013. *Best of KQ: Instructional Partnerships: A Pathway to Leadership.* Chicago: American Association of School Librarians.

Riggs, Donald E. 2001. "The Crisis and Opportunities in Library Leadership." *Journal of Library Administration* 32(3/4): 5–17.

Rojas, Carlos, and Glorya Wornum. 2018. "Speaking Up and Walking Out: Boston Students Fight for Education Justice." In *Lift Us Up, Don't Push Us Out: Voices from the Front Lines of the Educational Justice Movement,* ed. Mark R. Warren, 20–28. Boston: Beacon Press.

Senge, Peter, Nelda Cambron-McCabe, Timothy Lucas, Bryan Smith, Janis Dutton, and Art Kleiner. 2012. *Schools That Learn: A Fifth Discipline Fieldbook for Educators, Parents, and Everyone Who Cares about Education.* New York: Crown Business.

Todd, Ross J., Carol A. Gordon, and Ya-Ling Lu. 2012. "Clone the School Librarian: Evidence of the Role of the School Librarian in Professional Development." In *Growing Schools: Librarians as Professional Developers,* ed. D. Abilock, K. Fontichiaro, and V. H. Harada, xxi–xxiii. Santa Barbara, CA: Libraries Unlimited.

Glossary

advocacy
Advocacy is an ongoing process that results in actions taken by individuals or groups with the goal of influencing decision makers toward a preferred outcome.

agency
In education, agency involves students having an active role in and ownership over learning. They may set goals that are relevant and meaningful to their lives, practice autonomy by having voice and choice, and be empowered to share, reflect on, and grow through their learning.

ally
An ally is one who supports the efforts of another in the face of a common struggle or as they move toward a common goal.

Banned Books Week
First launched in the 1980s, Banned Books Week is an annual event, typically held during the last week of September and with one day designated as Banned Websites Day. It celebrates the freedom to read and serves as a means for raising awareness and educating people about the harms of censorship.

BIPOC/BISOC
BIPOC stands for Black, Indigenous, People of Color, and BISOC stands for Black, Indigenous, Students of Color.

collaboration
Collaboration for instruction involves coplanning, coteaching, and coassessing student learning outcomes with one or more members of the teaching faculty. Collaborating educators may also share responsibility for literacy and other events, policies, procedures, and practices.

community
A community is created when the people living in the same area interact with one another and have shared experiences and environments.

confidence
Confidence is a feeling of self-assurance arising from a belief that we have the necessary support and resources.

cooperation
Compared with collaboration, cooperation tends to be more informal, short term, and often lacks focused planning. Providing classroom teachers with a cart of resources or a librarian-created pathfinder are examples of cooperation.

coordination
Coordination requires more communication than cooperation, but unlike collaboration, each educator maintains their own authority. Teaching the same skill or strategy in the library while it's being taught in the classroom is an example of coordination.

coteaching
Coteaching involves two or more educators who have coplanned instruction and take one or more coteaching approaches, such as team teaching or center rotation teaching, to implement instruction.

culturally responsive
In education, being culturally responsive means learning from, honoring, and meaningfully including the multiple cultures in our educational spaces. It also means recognizing the strengths of our students' families and communities.

culture
Culture is composed of shared beliefs, knowledge, attitudes, language, behaviors, social interactions, and more. Cultures are created by people; they are dynamic.

curation
Curation is the act of collecting, organizing, and aligning resources for a specific purpose. For school librarians, this alignment is most often with the classroom curriculum.

curriculum
Curriculum includes the content, lessons, scope, and sequence of study.

diversity
According to ALA's Office for Diversity, Literacy and Outreach Services (ODLOS), diversity can be defined as the sum of the ways that people are both alike and different.

equality
Equality is the idea that all are afforded the same rights, privileges, and opportunities.

equity
According to the ODLOS, equity assumes difference and takes difference into account to ensure a fair process and, ultimately, a fair (or equitable) outcome.

inclusion

An inclusive school values and respects the cultures of all members of the learning community and creates a sense of belonging for all.

intellectual freedom

Intellectual freedom is the right of every individual to both seek and receive information from all points of view without restriction. Rooted in U.S. law, intellectual freedom is further supported through library professional standards and guidance, and involves protecting the rights of access, choice, privacy, and confidentiality.

leadership

School librarian leadership is the ability to influence the school community on the access and use of information and other resources to meet the needs and values of the school for the sake of improving the quality of learning for all.

liberatory

In *Pedagogy of the Oppressed*, Paolo Freire (2000) contrasted the potential for education to be oppressive or liberatory. Liberatory education empowers learners as humans, removing the hierarchy between teacher and student, valuing the knowledge of students' own experiences, and allowing them the freedom to critically question the truth of reality in order to be liberated.

marketing

Marketing involves tools and strategies to access library patrons' needs; it results in actions taken to meet those needs.

Office for Intellectual Freedom (OIF)

Established in 1967, the OIF is an ALA unit that implements policies related to intellectual freedom. OIF creates and provides guidance in the form of resources and services to educate librarians and the general public about intellectual freedom in libraries.

#OwnVoices

#OwnVoices is a hashtag originated by young adult author Corinne Duyvis to describe titles where the author and protagonist share a marginalized identity.

public relations

Public relations is one-way communication that delivers messages to target audiences.

Universal Design for Learning (UDL)

UDL (CAST 2018) is a brain research–informed framework to improve teaching and optimize learning for all students.

vulnerability

Vulnerability as defined by author Dr. Brené Brown (2012) is the demonstration of "uncertainty, risk, and emotional exposure." School librarians who have confidence in their role are willing to share their vulnerability and increase their capacity for leadership.

References

Brown, Brené. 2012. *Daring Greatly: How the Courage to Be Vulnerable Transforms the Way We Live, Love, Parent, and Lead.* New York: Avery.

CAST. 2018. "Universal Design for Learning Guidelines version 2.2." Available at https://udlguidelines.cast.org. Accessed December 28, 2020.

Freire, Paulo. 2000. *Pedagogy of the Oppressed.* New York: Continuum.

Notes: Spotlight Quotes

Introduction

Dr. Carol Gordon, Principal of Gordon Consulting and Retired Associate Professor, Rutgers The State University of New Jersey

> Gordon, C. A. 2017. "Assessing Access in School Libraries: Developing Meaningful Use of Library Resources and Services." *Synergy* 15(2). Available at https://www.slav.vic.edu.au/index.php/Synergy/article/view/v152201710/45. Accessed October 1, 2020.

Jen Gilbert, K–12 School Librarian, Eminence Independent Schools, Kentucky, and **James Allen**, Statewide School Library Lead, Kentucky Department of Education

> Gilbert, Jen, and James Allen. 2020. "One-Question Survey: What's Your Most Important Core Value?" *School Library Connection* (January/February) 36.

Talmudic Saying (cited in Friedman)

> Friedman, Thomas L. 2016. *Thank You for Being Late: An Optimist's Guide to Thriving in the Age of Acceleration.* New York: Farrar, Straus and Giroux.

Chapter 1

National Education Association, U.S. Education Employees Professional Organization

> National Education Association. n.d. "Diversity Toolkit: Social Justice." Available at http://www.nea.org//tools/30414.htm. Accessed October 1, 2020.

Mary Keeling, Library Services Supervisor, Newport News, Virginia, and Former AASL President

Keeling, Mary. 2019. "Providing Structures for Learning and Change." *Knowledge Quest* (blog), September 17. Available at https://knowledge quest.aasl.org/providing-structures-for-learning-and-change-equity -diversity-and-inclusion. Accessed October 1, 2020.

Jason Reynolds, Author and National Ambassador for Young People's Literature

Reynolds, Jason. 2020. Speech. Presented at the Texas Library Association 2020 Virtual Conference, April 21.

Dr. Kafi Kumasi, Associate Professor, Library and Information Science, Wayne State University, Detroit, Michigan

Hansen, Joe. 2014. "Check It Out! Want Help Boosting Cultural Responsiveness at Your School? Ask Your Librarian." *Learning for Justice* 48 (Fall). Available at https://www.learningforjustice.org/magazine/fall-2014/check-it-out. Accessed February 16, 2021.

Chapter 2

Taun Wright, CEO of EqualRead.org

Wright, Taun. 2015. "Why Do We Need Diverse Books in Non-Diverse Schools?" *The Open Book* (blog), March 25. Available at http://blog .leeandlow.com/2015/03/25/why-do-we-need-diverse-books-in -non-diverse-schools. Accessed October 1, 2020.

Chimamanda Adichie, Novelist and Short Story Author

Adichie, Chimamanda. 2009. "The Danger of a Single Story." *TEDGlobal* (video), July. Available at https://www.ted.com/talks/chimamanda _ngozi_adichie_the_danger_of_a_single_story?language=en. Accessed October 1, 2020.

Malinda Lo, Young Adult Books Author

Lo, Malinda. 2015. "Perceptions of Diversity in Book Reviews." *Malinda Lo* (blog), February 19. Available at https://www.malindalo.com /blog/2015/02/perceptions-of-diversity-in-book-reviews. Accessed October 1, 2020.

Nessa, Lawton, Oklahoma

Personal Communication, Google Meet, August 22, 2020.

Chapter 3

Kiah Morris, Former Vermont State Representative and Current Movement Politics Director at Rights & Democracy Vermont

Morris, Kiah. 2019. "Three Tools for Anyone Serious about Radical Diversity." *TEDxStowe* (video), May 31. Available at https://youtu.be /UPfdAX—6ME. Accessed October 1, 2020.

Dr. R. David Lankes, Director of the University of South Carolina School of Library and Information Science

> American Library Association. 2018. "Are Libraries Neutral?" *American Libraries.* Available at https://americanlibrariesmagazine.org/2018 /06/01/are-libraries-neutral. Accessed October 1, 2020.

Dr. Paul Gorski, Founder and Lead Equity Specialist at the Equity Literacy Institute

> Gorski, Paul, ed. 2020. "About Equity Literacy." *Equity Literacy Institute.* Available at https://www.equityliteracy.org/equity-literacy. Accessed October 1, 2020.

Dr. Jamila Lyiscott, Spoken Word Poet, Assistant Professor of Social Justice Education at the University of Massachusetts Amherst, and a Senior Research Fellow of Teachers College, Columbia University's Institute for Urban and Minority Education

> Lyiscott, Jamila. 2019. *Black Appetite. White Food. Issues of Race, Voice, and Justice within and beyond the Classroom.* New York: Routledge.

Hazel Edwards, LGBTQIA+ Activist, Educator at the Attic Youth Center

> Lindberg, Maya. 2017. "Nothing about Us without Us Is for Us." *Learning for Justice,* Fall. Available at https://www.learningforjustice .org/magazine/fall-2017/nothing-about-us-without-us-is-for-us. Accessed February 16, 2021.

Chapter 4

Helen R. Adams, Former School Librarian and Online Senior Lecturer at Antioch University–Seattle

> Adams, Helen R. 2013. *Protecting Intellectual Freedom and Privacy in Your School Library.* Santa Barbara, CA: ABC-CLIO.

Dr. Shannon Oltmann, Assistant Professor, School of Information Science, University of Kentucky

> Oltmann, Shannon. 2017. "Creating Space at the Table: Intellectual Freedom Can Bolster Diverse Voices." *Library Quarterly: Information, Community, Policy* 87(4): 410–418.

Pat Scales, Retired School Librarian and Author of Bimonthly *School Library Journal* Column "Scales on Censorship"

> Scales, Pat. 2009. Quoted in "A Dirty Little Secret: Self-Censorship." *School Library Journal.* Available at https://www.slj.com/?detail Story=a-dirty-little-secret-self-censorship. Accessed October 1, 2020.

Barbara M. Jones, Previous Director ALA Office for Intellectual Freedom and Executive Director Freedom to Read Foundation

Jones, Barbara M. 2015. "What Is Intellectual Freedom?" In *Intellectual Freedom Manual*, 9th ed., ed. T. Magi, 3–13. Chicago: American Library Association.

Chapter 5

Shelby Denhof, High School Educator, Rockford, Michigan

Denhof, Shelby. 2016. "Building Relationships with Students through Books." *Cult of Pedagogy* (blog). Available at https://www.cultof pedagogy.com/ya-middle-school-books. Accessed October 1, 2020.

Hilda K. Weisburg, Author, Blogger, and Retired School Librarian, New Jersey

Weisburg, Hilda K. 2019. "Building Relationships with Students." *On Libraries* (blog). Available at https://hildakweisburg.com/2019/08 /26/on-libraries-building-relationships-with-students. Accessed October 1, 2020.

Darcy McNee, Teacher-Librarian, North Saanich Middle School, British Columbia, and **Dr. Elaine Radmer**, Gonzaga University, Spokane, Washington

McNee, Darcy, and Elaine Radmer. 2017. "Librarians and Learning: The Impact of Collaboration." *English Leadership Quarterly* 40(1): 6–9.

Donna Mignardi, School Librarian, Calvert High School, and **Jennifer Sturge**, Teacher Specialist for School Libraries and Instructional Technology, Calvert County, Maryland

Mignardi, Donna, and Jennifer Sturge. 2018. "Sneaky Tactics." *Programming Library* (blog). Available at https://programminglibrarian.org /blog/sneaky-tactics. Accessed October 1, 2020.

Chapter 6

Dr. Brian R. Miller, Superintendent, Pine-Richland School District, Pennsylvania

Miller, Brian R. 2020. In discussion with the author. August.

Dr. Ken Haycock, Professor Emeritus and Former Director of the School of Information at San José State University

Haycock, Ken. 2017. "Leadership from the Middle Building Influence for Change." In *The Many Faces of School Library Leadership,* ed. S. Coatney and V. H. Harada, 1–12. Santa Barbara, CA: Libraries Unlimited.

Dr. Audrey Church, Professor, Longwood University, Virginia

Church, Audrey P. 2008. "The Instructional Role of the Library Media Specialist as Perceived by Elementary School Principals." *School Library Media Research* 11. Available at http://www.ala.org/aasl

/sites/ala.org.aasl/files/content/aaslpubsandjournals/slr/vol11 /SLMR_InstructionalRole_V11.pdf. Accessed October 1, 2020.

Carolyn Foote, Technolibrarian, Westlake High School and Eanes ISD District Librarian, Austin, Texas
Foote, Carolyn. 2015. "The Librarian—Principal Relationship." *Teacher Librarian* 42(4): 27–28.

Chapter 7

Audre Lorde, Writer, Feminist, Librarian, and Civil Rights Activist
Lorde, Audre. 2020. *When I Dare to Be Powerful.* New York: Penguin.

Dr. Margaret J. Wheatley, Author, Speaker, Teacher, Community Worker, and Leader
Wheatley, Margaret J. 2017. *Who Do We Choose to Be? Facing Reality, Claiming Leadership, Restoring Sanity.* San Francisco: Berrett-Koehler.

Chögyam Trungpa, Scholar, Teacher, Author, Poet, and Tibetan Buddhist Meditation Master
Trungpa, Chögyam. 1998. *Timely Rain: Selected Poetry of Chögyam Trungpa.* Boston: Random House.

Dr. Brené Brown, Researcher, Author, Speaker, and Storyteller
Brown, Brené. 2010. "The Power of Vulnerability." *TEDxHouston* (video), June. Available at https://www.ted.com/talks/brene_brown_the _power_of_vulnerability. Accessed October 1, 2020.

Iris Eichenlaub, Librarian/Technology Integrator
Personal communication.

Rachael Kessler, Author, Speaker, and Teacher
Kessler, Rachael. 2000. *The Soul of Education: Helping Students Find Connection, Compassion, and Character at School.* Alexandria, VA: ASCD Publications.

Dinos Christianopoulos, Poet, Scholar, and Literary Critic
Christianopoulos, Dinos. 1995. *Poems.* Translated and with an introduction by Nicholas Kostis.

Chapter 8

Cherity Pennington, District-Level Communications and Library Services Coordinator, Shawnee, Oklahoma
Pennington, Cherity. 2020. "The Future of Education Needs School Librarians." *Knowledge Quest* (blog), May 11. Available at https:// knowledgequest.aasl.org/the-future-of-education-needs-school -librarians. Accessed October 1, 2020.

Steve Tetreault, English Language Arts Teacher, Certified School Librarian, Holmdel New Jersey

> Tetreault, Steve. 2019. "Themes in School Librarianship: Advocacy Part 1." *Knowledge Quest* (blog), October 10. Available at https://knowledge quest.aasl.org/themes-in-school-librarianship-part-1-advocacy. Accessed October 1, 2020.

Len Bryan, Manager of Library Technical Systems, Denver Public Schools, Colorado

> Bryan, Len. 2020. "Gathering and Visualizing Quantitative School Library Data." *Knowledge Quest* (blog), February 5. Available at https://knowledgequest.aasl.org/data-informed-library-advocacy -from-aasl19-part-2. Accessed October 1, 2020.

Kathryn Roots Lewis, Past-President of AASL, Former District-Level School Library Supervisor, Norman, Oklahoma

> Lewis, Kathryn Roots. 2020. "School Administrators and the Power of School Librarians." *Knowledge Quest* (blog), April 29. Available at https://knowledgequest.aasl.org/school-administrators-and-the -power-of-school-librarians. Accessed October 1, 2020.

Chapter 9

George Couros, Educator, and Innovative Teaching, Learning, and Leadership Consultant

> Couros, George. 2015. *The Innovator's Mindset: Empower Learning, Unleash Talent, and Lead in a Culture of Creativity.* San Diego: Dave Burgess Consulting.

Representative John Lewis, American Politician, Civil Rights Leader

> Lewis, John. 2020. *BrainyQuote.com.* Available at https://www.brainyquote .com/quotes/john_lewis_810325. Accessed October 1, 2020.

Simon Sinek, Author and Motivational Speaker

> Sinek, Simon. 2009. *Start with Why: How Great Leaders Inspire Everyone to Take Action.* New York: Penguin.

Dr. Alan Kay, American Computer Scientist

> Kay, Alan. 1971. PARC, Palo Alto Research Center Meeting. Palo Alto: California.

About the Contributors

Stacy Allen, MA, serves as assistive technology specialist for Calvert County Public Schools in Maryland. She has worked in special education for twenty-five years. Her current position allows her to focus on equity and access for students with disabilities through work with teachers, students, and families. Stacy has been in love with books forever and spends as much time as possible in libraries and bookstores. She is an active member of the Society for Children's Book Writers and Illustrators (SCBWI) from whom she received a Work in Progress Award in 2018. Her poem "Hungry" received Highlight's *High Five*™ magazine's Poem of the Year Award for 2015. Stacy is also the founding director of the nonprofit community art studio Bay Arts Center, Inc. She holds master of arts degrees from Towson University and from St. John's College, Annapolis. Connect with Stacy on Instagram and Twitter @artisfood, or see her work online at stacyallen.com.

Meg Boisseau Allison, MEd (she/her), is a teacher-librarian and social justice advocate at a public high school in Vermont. She has taught graduate courses in library media studies at the University of Vermont and presents widely at state and national conferences. As a Global Teacher Fellow, she traveled to France and Italy in 2013 to research fairy tales. She was recognized in 2013 as a Vermont Outstanding Teacher and honored with a Vermont House Concurrent Resolution, H.C.R 200. She served six years on Vermont's Dorothy Canfield Fisher Book Award Committee, the country's second oldest middle-grade book award. She's honored to share the Vermont School Library Association (VSLA) 2020 Outstanding School Librarian Award with chapter coauthor Peter Langella. She currently serves on the Vermont School Library Association's executive committee. She is an American Association of School Librarians (AASL) Social Media Superstar: Social Justice Defender finalist. Connect with her on Twitter @meg_allison and Instagram @u32library.

Anita Cellucci, MEd LMS, is a high school librarian, K–12 library leader, in Westborough, Massachusetts. She advises teens in a library advisory board and coaches a poetry spoken word team. As a teaching lecturer for Plymouth State University, New Hampshire, she teaches children's and young adult literature with a focus on social justice and diversity. Anita serves on the AASL Board of Directors, past Massachusetts School Library Association (MSLA) Advocacy cochair, and past MSLA president. Anita has published articles in the *School Library Journal* and *Teacher Librarian,* is a columnist for *School Library Connection's* "Full Voice," and wrote a chapter for the book *Guided Inquiry Design in Action: High School.* She is the recipient of the MSLA Peggy Hallisey Leadership Award 2020, MSLA Service Award 2017, AASL Social Media Superstar Finalist, 2018, Social Justice Defender Category, 2019 LJ Mover & Shaker, and received the SLJ & Scholastic School Librarian of the Year 2016 Co-Finalist Award. linktr.ee/anitacellucci.

TuesD Chambers, MEd, serves as a teacher-librarian at Ballard High School in Seattle Public Schools. An educator for over twenty years, she earned her MEd in professional development and leadership with a media library endorsement. TuesD teaches digital leadership, literacy, and 21st-century skills to students and was chosen as the Washington State Teacher Librarian of the Year for 2019. She leads multiple technology initiatives including the Digital Learning Librarian Ambassadors and Instructional Innovation Cohort. TuesD has presented at the International Society for Technology Education (ISTE), South by Southwest Education Conference, and Oculus Connect 6 about the intentional use of technology to impact learning and school culture. A firm believer in the power of collaboration, she works with teachers and librarians to create student-centered classrooms in her role as a content library specialist. Find TuesD on Twitter @BeaverReaders or Instagram at @beaverreadersbhs; she loves to connect with other passionate educational leaders.

Kelly Gustafson, MEd, serves as the Wexford Elementary School principal in the Pine-Richland School District in Pennsylvania. With more than twenty years of experience as an administrator, Kelly credits professional, collaborative relationships formed with school librarians and teachers as motivators to advocate for all children having access to books. Kelly's passion for school library partnerships fueled her active role in AASL's School Leader Collaborative. She champions the value of librarians as a member of AASL and Pennsylvania School Librarians Association. Kelly participated in ALA National Legislative Days, testified before the Pennsylvania House of Representatives Education Committee, and contributed to the *Guidelines for Pennsylvania School Library Programs* (2019). Experience as a special educator, adjunct professor, and practicing principal drives her advocacy action steps to lead workshops, author publications, and share her voice to build a community of readers. Connect with her on Twitter @GustafsonkKelly.

Pam Harland, EdD, served as a librarian for twenty-five years working in schools, public libraries, academic libraries, and at the Federal Reserve Bank of Boston. She is now a member of the faculty at Plymouth State University in New Hampshire where she directs the school librarian and digital learning specialist educator preparation programs. Pam served in several leadership positions at the state level in New Hampshire and on the AASL Board of Directors. She was awarded New Hampshire's Elsie Domingo Service Award in 2016, New Hampshire's School Librarian of the Year Award in 2010, and New Hampshire's Intellectual Freedom Award in 2009. Pam authored *The Learning Commons: Seven Simple Steps to Transform Your Library* (Libraries Unlimited 2011). Most recently she earned her doctorate in Educational Leadership in 2019 in which she researched the leadership behaviors of school librarians. Connect with her on Twitter @pamlibrarian.

Nancy Jo Lambert, MLS, is a Google certified trainer with friEdtechnology and high school teacher–librarian at Reedy High School in Frisco, Texas. She has her MLS from the University of North Texas. She is a presenter advocating for libraries by telling the story of the learning happening in her library. She has held and holds positions in the Texas Library Association, Texas Association of School Librarians, ALA, AASL, and TCEA (Texas Computer Education Association). She was named TCEA Library Media Specialist of the Year and the AASL Social Media Superstar Curriculum Champion in 2019. She is also a cisgender, White, bisexual educator and cofounder of #TeachPride and EduPrideAlliance. She is known for sharing her professional work from her library on Twitter @NancyJoLambert and on her websites: reedylibrary.com and nancyjolambert.com.

Peter Patrick Langella, MFA (he/him), is a librarian and social justice advisor at a high school in Vermont. He earned a master of fine arts in writing for children and young adults from Vermont College of Fine Arts. Peter also works as a school library instructor at the University of Vermont, and an English instructor at Northern Vermont University. He was a 2017 Fellow at the Rowland Foundation, a member of the first AASL Induction Leadership Cohort, and the corecipient of the VSLA's 2020 Outstanding School Librarian Award with chapter coauthor Meg Boisseau Allison. Peter is currently in his three-year executive term on the VSLA Board and simultaneously serves as its legislative concerns representative. Peter is also the cofounder and co-organizer of Teen Lit Mob Vermont, the state's only teen literary festival. Connect with him on Twitter @PeterLangella.

Erika Long, MSIS, an alumna of the University of Tennessee Knoxville, is a school librarian in Tennessee. Erika is a member of ALA, AASL, Tennessee Library Association (TLA), and the Tennessee Association of School Librarians (TASL). She serves on the board of AASL and TLA, was part of the ALA Presidential Initiative: Fight for School Libraries, AASL Presidential Initiative Task Force on Equity, Diversity, and Inclusion, ALA's United Nations 2030 Sustainable Development Goals Task Force, the University of Tennessee Knoxville SIS Alumni Advisory Board, and other committees. Erika has had the privilege of presenting at state and national conferences. She previously blogged for *The Horn Book* and TASL Talks and has a vignette in *Promoting African American Writers: Library Partnerships for Outreach, Programming, and Literacy* (Libraries Unlimited, forthcoming). She has twice been named an AASL Social Media Superstar finalist. Connect with her on Twitter @erikaslong and Instagram @notyomamaslibrarian.

Dan McDowell, MA, is the director of learning and innovation in the Grossmont Union High School District (GUSHD), San Diego County, California. During the COVID-19 crisis, he coordinated the spring and fall 2020 GUHSD district learning plans. His other current district projects include a districtwide rollout of Universal Design for Learning (UDL), facilitating an exploration of cultural competency, and organizing professional learning for teachers and administrators. Previously, Dan served as the director of instructional technology, where he planned and implemented the 1:1 FutureForward Chromebook program with a strong focus on teaching and learning. Before his administrative work, he taught high school social studies and photography at West Hills High School for eighteen years. Dan has been involved in technology staff development since 1996, leading over two hundred workshops and presentations. He is a Google Certified Innovator (Santa Monica, 2007) and teaches graduate-level educational technology courses in the School of Education at San Diego State University.

Judi Moreillon, PhD, is a literacies and libraries consultant. She began teaching preservice school librarians in 1995. Her research and publications focus on school librarian leadership and classroom teacher–school librarian instructional partnerships. A former classroom teacher, literacy coach, and classroom teacher educator, Judi served as a collaborating school librarian at all three instructional levels. She is the author of four other professional books for school librarians and four books for children and families. She earned the 2019 Scholastic Publishing Award. Judi served as a mentor for the Lilead Project, currently serves as cochair of the Teacher Librarian Division of the Arizona Library Association, and recently chaired the American Association of School Librarians Reading Position Statements Task Force. She earned both an MLS and a PhD in education at the University of Arizona.

Judi's homepage is storytrail.com. She blogs at schoollibrarianleadership .com and tweets @CactusWoman.

Stephanie Powell, MEITE, is a librarian at Green Level High School in Wake County, North Carolina. A National Board-Certified Teacher and life-long learner, she has been a classroom teacher and now librarian for nearly twenty-eight years. She earned a master's in instructional technology from UNC–Chapel Hill and her master's in library and information science from UNC-Greensboro. Stephanie is invested in promoting equity and being an advocate for underrepresented voices through library services.

Suzanne Sannwald, MLIS (she/her), has worked as a high school teacher-librarian since 2014. She builds on her previous education-related roles from middle school to higher education levels, serving as a certificated classroom teacher, classified library technician, district library supervisor, and student affairs technology manager. Suzanne earned both an MA in teaching and learning with technology and an MLIS. She was a 2015–2016 ALA Spectrum Scholar, 2016 California School Library Association Leadership for Diversity Scholar, 2017 school site Golden Apple Teacher of the Year, 2018–2019 AASL Induction Program member, San José State University iSchool lecturer start-ing fall 2020, and *School Library Connection* contributor. Suzanne has pub-lished articles and presented on topics including user experience, information literacy, collaboration, advocacy, and affirming students' reading and larger lives. Connect with her on Twitter @suzannesannwald.

M. E. Shenefiel, MLIS (she/her), is the librarian at Eden Hall Upper Elemen-tary School in the Pine-Richland School District (Gibsonia, Pennsylvania), where she also serves as the library department chairperson and a building level technology coach. Former president of the Beaver County Association of School Librarians (Pennsylvania), she is currently an active committee member in several professional organizations, including the Western Penn-sylvania School Librarians Association, the Pennsylvania School Librarians Association, and the American Association of School Librarians. She was a contributor to both the *Guidelines for Pennsylvania School Library Programs* (2019) and *The Model Curriculum for Learners in Pennsylvania School Libraries* (2019). M. E. received her master of library and information science degree from the University of Pittsburgh in 2001. Connect with her on Twitter @bookbird.

Suzanne Sherman, MIS, is a former English and Spanish teacher turned librarian. She has been a school librarian for fourteen years and is currently the librarian at Hardin Valley Academy, a public high school in Knox County, Tennessee. She earned her MIS from the University of Tennessee Knoxville

(2007) and has been a lecturer for the UTK School of Information Sciences for thirteen years, teaching both undergraduate and graduate students in the field of children's and young adult literature. She focuses much of her work at Hardin Valley Academy on collaborating with classroom teachers and developing lessons with them that drive the students toward inquiry. She is a member of the board for the UTK Center for Children's and Young Adult Literature. Suzanne is currently serving as a coeditor for *The ALAN* (Assembly on Literature for Adolescents) *Review*, a publication of the National Council of Teachers of English (NCTE).

Kristin Fraga Sierra, MEd, is the teacher-librarian at Lincoln High School in Tacoma, Washington. She has been an educator for thirteen years— eight years overseas and five years in secondary school libraries in Tacoma. Kristin is advisor of Project Lit Abes Book Club, a chapter of Project Lit Community, and she has an MEd and endorsement in Library Media. She is an alumnus of Antioch University. She is on Tacoma's Library Leadership committee and as a Microsoft Innovator in Education leader. A member of ALA, AASL, Washington Library Association, and REFORMA, she has presented at an SLJ Summit and NCCE conferences. She is published in *School Library Journal* and AASL's *Knowledge Quest*. Kristin is on the AASL Engagement Committee and the Evergreen Teen Books Awards Committee. As the daughter of a Cuban refugee, wife and mother to Honduran citizens, Kristin is a proud member of the Latin American community. Connect on Instagram and Twitter @lincolnabesread or her blog at lincolnabesread.wordpress.com.

Julie Stivers, MLIS (she/her/hers), is the librarian at Mount Vernon Middle, an alternative public school in Raleigh, North Carolina. Her work has been published in *Knowledge Quest*, *School Library Journal*, and *YALS*. As a 2018 ALA Emerging Leader, she helped develop AASL's *Defending Intellectual Freedom: LGBTQ+ Materials in School Libraries*. She is the recipient of AASL's 2017 Frances Henne Award and was named a 2019 *Library Journal* Mover and Shaker. She served as the chair for the YALSA Presidential Taskforce: Youth Activism through Community Engagement and is a facilitator in her district's Office of Equity Affairs Summer Writing Institute for high school students. Her research and practical interests include culturally sustaining pedagogy, building inclusive library spaces, and exploring the power of graphic novels, manga, and anime with her students. She earned her MLIS from SILS at UNC–Chapel Hill and connects on Twitter at @BespokeLib.

Jennifer Sturge, MEd (she/hers), is employed by Calvert County Public Schools. She has an undergraduate degree in education from Clarion University, a master's in school library and instructional technology from Mansfield University, and is currently a doctoral student at Point Park University. She has been an educator for twenty-seven years, and a proponent of both school and public libraries since she won the Calvert Library bookmark creation contest at the age of seven. Jennifer is a 2017–2018 Lilead Fellow, the Maryland Technology Leader of the Year for 2019, and is the 2020–2021 Maryland Association of School Librarians President. She is currently a blogger for *Programming Librarian* with colleague Donna Mignardi. She also blogs for *Knowledge Quest* on a regular basis. Jennifer is an adjunct professor at the iSchool for the University of Maryland College Park. She resides in southern Maryland with her family. Connect with her on Twitter @sturgej.

Sandy Walker, MA, serves as the supervisor of equity and school improvement for Calvert County Public Schools. He works with school administration, staff, and students to establish an identity-safe learning and working environment where success is not predetermined by income, zip code, or race. During his twenty-three years in education, he has been a classroom teacher, a teacher-trainer, and an education program instructor. He is driven by a passion for equipping students with the knowledge and skills necessary for discovering and valuing their own voice. He earned a master's of arts and humanities from the University at Buffalo and an administrative certification from McDaniel College.

Index